# Fodor's
# 25Best

# NEW YORK CITY

# Contents

## INTRODUCING NEW YORK     4

An overview of the city and its history, as well as top tips on making the most of your stay.

## TOP 25     12

We've pulled together the Top 25 must-see sights and experiences in New York.

## MORE TO SEE     64

Even more options for great places to visit if you have plenty of time to spend in the city, whether it's in the city center or farther afield.

## CITY TOURS     76

We've broken the city into areas with recommended tours in each one to help you get the best from your visit.

## SHOP     114

Discover some of New York's best shops and what they have to offer, from local produce to high fashion to books.

## KEY TO SYMBOLS

- 🚩 Map reference to the accompanying pull-out map
- ⊠ Address
- ☎ Telephone number
- ◷ Opening/closing times
- 🍴 Restaurant or café
- Ⓜ Nearest subway (Metro) station
- 🚌 Nearest bus route
- 🚆 Nearest rail station

## ENTERTAINMENT 126

Whether you're after a cultural fix or just want a place to relax with a drink after a hard day's sightseeing, we've made the best choices for you.

## EAT 138

Uncover great dining experiences, from a quick bite for lunch to top-notch evening meals.

## SLEEP 150

We've brought together the best hotels in the city, whatever budget you're on.

## NEED TO KNOW 160

The practical information you need to make your trip run smoothly.

## PULL-OUT MAP

The pull-out map with this book is a comprehensive street plan of the city. We've given grid references within the book for each sight and listing.

- 🚢 Nearest riverboat or ferry stop
- ♿ Facilities for visitors with disabilities
- ℹ️ Tourist information
- ❓ Other practical information
- 🖐 Admission charges: Expensive (over $12), Moderate ($5–$12) and Inexpensive (under $5)
- ▷ Further information

# Introducing New York

"New York is an island off the coast of Europe." There's a lot of truth in this witticism, and it's no wonder this is the city most overseas visitors choose first. The qualities that weld New Yorkers to the city also distinguish them from most Americans.

Residents of Manhattan value directness, diversity and creativity; they live at a ridiculous pace; they work all hours (they have to, to pay the rent); they walk—fast—everywhere; they fail to keep their opinions to themselves; they have street smarts; they are capital L Liberal. New York is a key Blue State, having voted Democrat in the last seven presidential elections. The city that actually lived through the 9/11 attack that kicked off an era of paranoia and xenophobia refuses to give in to fear; New Yorkers have all the chutzpah they ever did.

In New York, where some hip neighborhood is forever preparing to eclipse the last hot spot, change is the only constant. The crime-ridden, graffiti-scarred mean streets of the late 20th century are all but a distant memory. In fact, these days New York is the safest large city in America (at least according to the NYPD). In stark contrast to the gritty days, you'll see strollers wherever you go, because there is a mini baby-boom in progress. Real estate prices are in the realm of fiction, and a whole lot of regular folks have decamped for Brooklyn, while those who can't afford Brooklyn have gone to Queens. These days parts of Harlem are glamorous and beautiful; the Bronx is next. Staten Island, the fifth borough that most visitors know only for its ferry, is the final frontier.

For many, Manhattan will always be the center of the universe. It's where deals are done, stars are born, legends—and fortunes—are made. Nowhere else in America offers such diversity in fashion, food, design, theater and the arts. The constant stimulation is addictive, and simply being here is worth a thousand inconveniences. You can take in only so much of the big picture in one visit. So do as New Yorkers do—find a corner of the city and make it your own.

## FACTS AND FIGURES

- Visitors in 2015: 58.3 million (a new record)
- Dollars spent by visitors in 2014: $61 billion
- Hotel rooms by end 2015: 102,000
- Population in 2015: 8.5 million
- Licensed yellow cabs: 13,600
- Feature films shot in New York: more than 250 a year

## REAL ESTATE

New York is in the midst of a building boom, with luxury skyscrapers that are among the tallest—and most expensive—in the world. This has put the squeeze on some middle-class New Yorkers. Still, many residents view their homes as not just their castles, but as their portfolio, their retirement plan and their chief financial burden.

## BROOKLYN

Once a separate city, the vast borough of Brooklyn across the East River has experienced a migration of disaffected Manhattanites that has changed its character forever. Previously, Brooklyn wasn't trendy; now it's a destination for excellent restaurants, good music venues and great parties in those oh-so-desirable brownstones.

## ONE WORLD TRADE CENTER

Nicknamed the Freedom Tower, the new tower in the World Trade Center (▷ 62–63) is officially called One World Trade Center (1WTC). It stands 1,776ft (541m) high—symbolic of the date of US independence—making it the tallest building in America. The stunning observatory opened to the public in spring 2015.

# Focus On Architecture

New York is constantly changing, and nowhere is this more apparent than in its architecture. Skyscrapers symbolize the city, but it has many other gems, from ornate art deco office lobbies to the classical columns, carvings and statuary of its Beaux Arts public buildings.

### Skyscrapers Past

Although Chicago erected the first skyscraper in 1885, New York embraced the high-rise building style so grandly that it has become the hallmark of the city's skyline. Among the earliest still standing is the 1899 Park Row Building, topped by its distinctive Beaux Arts domes, which at 391ft (119m) held the title of "world's tallest building" for nine years. Other notable early skyscapers include the 1902 Flatiron Building by Daniel Burnham (▷ 68); the 700ft (213m) Metropolitan Life Insurance Tower (1909), modeled after St. Mark's Campanile in Venice; and the neo-Gothic Woolworth Building (1913), at 792ft (241m) the world's tallest until1930.

In Lower Manhattan, skyscrapers grew so thick and fast that the streets of the Financial District started to turn into dark canyons. Zoning laws were passed in 1916, requiring builders to taper the upper storys with "setbacks" to allow light to reach ground level.

By 1930, the race for the top had become a battle of egos, as 40 Wall Street was trumped by the spire of the Chrysler Building (▷ 67), only to lose its title the following year to the Empire State Building (▷ 28–29). It remained the world's tallest building until the World Trade Center towers went up in 1972.

### ...and Present

From the 1950s onward, art deco elegance gave way to the glass "curtain wall" buildings of the International and Postmodern styles, which are so prominent in Midtown. The

*Clockwise from top left: Norman Foster's Hearst Tower; the triangular FlatIron Building; 19th-century Gramercy Park Historic District; interior of the US Custom House,*

21st century has seen the addition of such new landmarks to the city skyline as Norman Foster's Hearst Tower (2006), with its gleaming diagonal grid frame. When One World Trade Center (▷ 5) was completed in 2013, New York once again became home to the tallest building in the United States.

### Civic and Residential Architecture
But there's much more to New York architecture than these high-rise wonders. Outstanding among its civic buildings are several Beaux Arts beauties, including the US Custom House (1907; ▷ 73), the New York Public Library (1911; ▷ 48–49) and Grand Central Terminal (1913; ▷ 34–35). SoHo's Cast Iron Historic District (▷ 52–53) is lined with elaborate Italianate facades.

Residential architecture is also fascinating in this commercial city, from the brick tenements of the Lower East Side with their zigzagging fire escapes, to the fine brownstone town houses with their high stoops and elaborate doorways lining the leafy streets of Greenwich Village or Brooklyn Heights, to flamboyant luxury apartment buildings like the Ansonia and Dakota overlooking Central Park on the Upper West Side.

### Early Relics
Sadly, very little remains in Manhattan from the city's earliest days. Seek out the colonial-era St. Paul's Chapel (▷ 72), the Federal-style warehouses of Schermerhorn Row at South Street Seaport (▷ 72), The Row, a line of Greek Revival houses on the north side of Washington Square (▷ 73), or the delightful 19th-century houses surrounding Gramercy Park, once home to the likes of John Steinbeck (No. 38) and Joseph Pulitzer (No. 17). These survivors are gems in a city that is always tearing down the old to make room for the new in its never-ending reach for the stars.

*one of New York's finest Beaux Arts buildings; The Row, Washington Square North; the spire of the Chrysler Building; the Woolworth Building's neo-Gothic facade*

# Top Tips For…

These great suggestions will help you tailor your ideal visit to New York, no matter how you choose to spend your time.

### Star Chefs
Jean-Georges Vongerichten's restaurant (▷ 146) is the flagship of his ever-growing worldwide empire.
Daniel Boulud at **Café Boulud** will wow you (▷ 143). Be sure to try the madeleines.
At **Eleven Madison Park** (▷ 144–145) chef Daniel Humm is a master of reinvention, with the most complex tasting menus in the city.
For fish, nobody matches Eric Ripert at **Le Bernardin** (▷ 142).

### Being On Trend
Trot over to **Jeffrey New York** (▷ 122) to refresh your wardrobe, or, for vintage, **Resurrection** (▷ 124).
Get a taste of the LES at the **Parkside Lounge** (▷ 135).
Have a late supper at **The Spotted Pig** (▷ 149).
Check out the latest show at the **New Museum of Contemporary Art** (▷ 71) or go gallery hopping in **Chelsea** (▷ 66–67).

### Partying till Dawn
On Friday and Saturday dance the night away to Latin grooves at **SOB's** (▷ 137).
Go with the groove at the late-night jazz series at the **Blue Note** (▷ 132) from 12.30am on Friday and Saturday.
Ward off a hangover with a hearty breakfast or some Ukrainian soul food at **Veselka** (▷ 149), open 24 hours.

### Big and Beautiful Views
Harbor rooms at the **Ritz-Carlton Battery Park** (▷ 158) include a telescope.
Take in the lake view from Central Park's **Loeb Boathouse** (▷ 147).

*Clockwise from top left: Vintage style for sale; view from the Top of the Rock at the Rockefeller Center; tiger enclosure at the Bronx Zoo; head to the Blue Note for*

Not everyone knows about the **Roof Garden Café and Martini Bar at the Met** (▷ 136). **Top of the Rock** (▷ 51) rivals the **Empire State Building** (▷ 28–29) for views, but the **One World Observatory** (▷ 63) is the city's highest—you can see 50 miles (80km) on a clear day.

### Bringing the Kids
You can never go wrong with a good zoo. **Bronx Zoo** (▷ 74) is vast; the one in **Central Park** (▷ 18–19) won't take all day. Take them to **Serendipity 3** (▷ 149) for frozen hot chocolate.
Get tickets for **The New Victory Theater** (▷ 135).
You could spend days exploring the **American Museum of Natural History** (▷ 14), from dinosaur halls to the Space Theater.

### Classic NYC
See the ceiling, covered in toy trucks at the **'21' Club** (▷ 142).
**Bergdorf's, Saks** and **Bloomingdale's** are classic department stores with different personalities (▷ 120, 125).
The stunning **Chrysler Building** (▷ 67) is New York's favorite skyscraper and an art deco masterpiece.
Walk across the **Brooklyn Bridge** (▷ 66).

### Sporting Pursuits
If you are here during baseball season (April to September) **Yankee Stadium** (▷ 75) is a must. Or catch the Mets at Citi Field.
**Madison Square Garden** (▷ 134) has it all: Basketball (the Knicks), boxing, tennis, track and field, hockey, dog shows and more.
There's a game of something in progress in **Central Park** (▷ 18–19) all summer long. If it's winter, you can skate at **Wollman Rink**. Brooklyn's **Barclay's Center** is home to basketball and hockey (620 Atlantic Avenue).

*late-night jazz; the pedestrian walkway, Brooklyn Bridge; Madison Square Garden; the New Museum of Contemporary Art; Café Boulud, bastion of fine cuisine*

# Timeline

**Pre-1600** Native American groups populate New York area.

**1609** Henry Hudson sails up the Hudson River seeking the Northwest Passage.

**1625** "Nieuw Amsterdam" is founded by the Dutch West India Company on the tip of Manhattan Island. The following year the colony's leader purchases the island from the Native Americans for 60 guilders in trade goods.

## THE FIGHT FOR INDEPENDENCE

In 1664, Wall Street's wall failed to deter the British, who invaded Manhattan Island and named it New York. The first rumblings of Revolution came in 1765, when Stamp Act protesters rallied in Bowling Green Park. In 1770 the Sons of Liberty fought the British at the Battle of Golden Hill, and in 1776 the American Revolutionary War began and the British chose New York as their headquarters. The Declaration of Independence was read at City Hall Park in July 1776 and the Treaty of Paris ended the war in 1783.

**1664** In a bloodless coup, the British take over and rename the island New York.

**1776** American Revolutionary War begins.

**1785** New York becomes the capital of the United States (until 1790).

**1789** George Washington is sworn in as first US president at Federal Hall.

**1827** Slavery in New York is abolished.

**1845** Start of the first great waves of immigrants after the Irish Potato Famine.

**1863** Civil War Draft Riots divide the city.

**1868** The city's first "El" (elevated train) opens.

**1886** The Statue of Liberty is officially unveiled.

*Inauguration of George Washington on the balcony of Federal Hall in 1789*

*Immigrants arriving in New York Harbor, 1892*

**1892** Ellis Island immigration center opens.

**1904** The first subway opens.

**1929** The Great Depression follows the Wall Street Crash.

**1933** Prohibition ends after 14 years. Fiorello LaGuardia becomes mayor.

**1954** Ellis Island is closed down.

**1964** Race riots erupt in Harlem and Brooklyn.

**1975** A federal loan saves New York City from bankruptcy.

**1990** David Dinkins, New York's first black mayor, takes office.

**2001** Terrorists fly two hijacked planes into the World Trade Center, killing nearly 3,000 people.

**2011** The National September 11 Memorial opens at the World Trade Center Site.

**2012** The number of visitors to New York City in a single year exceeds 50 million for the first time.

**2013** The new tower at One World Trade Center becomes the tallest skyscraper in America.

**2016** January 23 becomes the snowiest day on record as severe blizzards strike the city.

### TENEMENT LIFE

As you make your first explorations in New York, consider how it was for the early immigrants, especially those who were herded through Ellis Island, then crammed into Lower East Side tenements. By the end of the 19th century, the immigrant neighborhoods were dominated by Italians and Eastern European Jews and had become the most densely populated place on earth. Many of these immigrants became garment workers in the ornate cast-iron buildings of SoHo, though many also sewed clothes at their overcrowded homes. Find out more at the Lower East Side Tenement Museum (▷ 68).

*Handouts during the Great Depression, following the Wall Street Crash of 1929*

*The Lower East Side Tenement Museum*

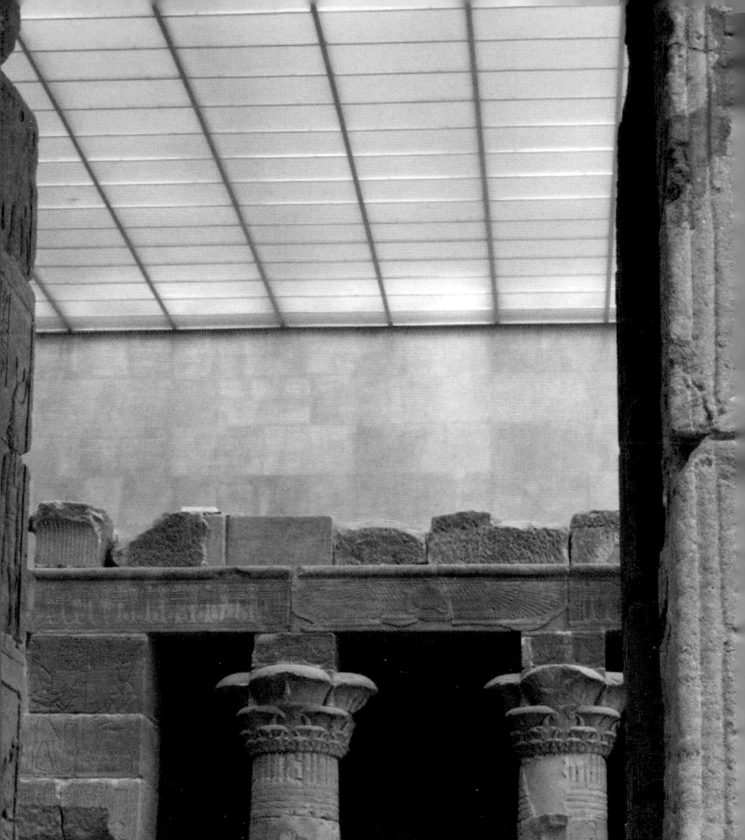

# Top 25

This section contains the must-see Top 25 sights and experiences in New York. They are listed alphabetically, and numbered so you can locate them on the inside front cover.

1. American Museum of Natural History     14
2. Brooklyn     16
3. Central Park     18
4. Chinatown     20
5. Cooper Hewitt Smithsonian Design Museum     22
6. East Village and NoHo     24
7. Ellis Island     26
8. Empire State Building     28
9. Fifth Avenue     30
10. Frick Collection     32
11. Grand Central Terminal     34
12. Greenwich Village     36
13. Guggenheim Museum     38
14. High Line     40
15. Lincoln Center     42
16. Metropolitan Museum of Art     44
17. Museum of Modern Art     46
18. New York Public Library     48
19. Rockefeller Center     50
20. SoHo     52
21. Statue of Liberty     54
22. Times Square     56
23. Wall Street     58
24. Whitney Museum of American Art     60
25. World Trade Center     62

TOP 25

# American Museum of Natural History

## HIGHLIGHTS

- Blue whale
- Titanosaur
- Cape York meteorite
- Dinosaur halls
- Journey to the Stars
- Star of India
- Animal dioramas
- Dinosaur embryo
- IMAX theater shows

## TIP

- You can observe the entire life cycle of tropical butterflies from October to June at the Butterfly Conservatory.

Of the 36 million items owned by the American Museum of Natural History—the largest such institution in the world—only a small fraction is on show. Don't miss the renowned dinosaur halls and stunning animal dioramas in native habitats.

**Star attractions** The original museum building opened in 1877 and, as it grew, its facade sported pink brownstone and granite towers, turrets and a grand Beaux Arts entrance on Central Park West. This opens into a soaring rotunda containing the museum's beloved Barosaurus, and visitors soon encounter the museum's prized Titanosaur cast (so enormous that its head extends into the hallway). The museum is best known for its splendid dinosaur halls, where real fossil specimens (rather

Left: The magnificent rotunda of the American Museum of Natural History is dominated by the skeleton of a Barosaurus; below: The stunning Rose Center for Earth and Space, adjoining the museum, includes the Hayden Planetarium, where space shows take place

than models) of an Apatosaurus and the first Tyrannosaurus rex ever exhibited are displayed. Another highlight is the enormous model of a blue whale looming over the Hall of Ocean Life. Equally impressive are the *tableaux morts* of animals from around the world, set in dioramas of great artistic merit.

**Gems and more** The 563-carat Star of India sapphire is part of the Morgan Memorial Hall of Gems, which contains merely a fraction of the museum's precious stones. There's far too much to see in one day, with four city blocks and the entire evolution of life on Earth covered. In the adjoining Rose Center for Earth and Space, a giant sphere contains the Big Bang Theater and the Hayden Planetarium, where thrilling space shows are projected on the dome.

## THE BASICS

amnh.org

➕ C6

✉ Central Park West/79th Street

☎ 212/769-5100

🕐 Daily 10–5.45

🍴 Various

Ⓑ B, C 81st Street–Museum of Natural History

🚌 M7, M10, M11, M79, M86

♿ Good

💲 Expensive

❓ 1-hour tours from 10.15 until 3.15. Call 212/769-5200 for advance reservations for special exhibits and events, including occasional sleepovers (some for children, others for adults only)

### HIGHLIGHTS

● Williamsburg
● Brooklyn Heights Promenade
● Bandshell concerts
● The Brooklyn Academy of Music (BAM)
● Brooklyn Museum of Art

### TIP

● New York Fun Tours runs Best of Brooklyn Multicultural Ethnic Neighborhood Food Tasting and Culture bus tours four times a week (newyorkfuntours.com).

Brooklyn has it all—one of the largest art museums in the US and some of New York's best restaurants; beaches and a park; a zoo, aquarium and children's museum; stylish neighborhoods and avant-garde arts.

**Big, bigger, biggest** If Brooklyn were still a separate city, it would be the fourth largest in the US. Home to more than 2.6 million people, it is the most populous of New York's boroughs, with Russian, Middle Eastern, Italian, West Indian, Hasidic Jewish and Chinese neighborhoods. The Brooklyn Museum of Art, intended by architects McKim, Mead & White to be the biggest museum in the world (it's actually the seventh largest in the US), has collections ranging from pre-Columbian art to 58 Rodin sculptures, plus what many feel are the best

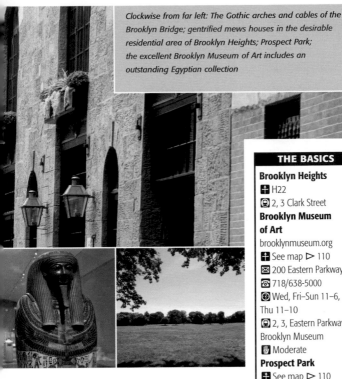

*Clockwise from far left: The Gothic arches and cables of the Brooklyn Bridge; gentrified mews houses in the desirable residential area of Brooklyn Heights; Prospect Park; the excellent Brooklyn Museum of Art includes an outstanding Egyptian collection*

Egyptian rooms outside Egypt and the British Museum. Steps from the museum's grand entrance is the Botanic Garden. Then, farther south, wander in Prospect Park, where summertime events and the zoo are highlights.

**The bridge and beyond** Brooklyn Bridge Park is an 85-acre (26ha) greenway reclaimed from derelict piers along the Brooklyn Heights waterfront, featuring jogging paths, water sports, and outdoor festivals. From Brooklyn Heights you can climb stairs to the Brooklyn Bridge pedestrian crossing or visit the Promenade for its view of Manhattan. Williamsburg is among the trendiest spots in the city, known for its restaurants, clubs, artisanal foods and crafts and, in warm weather, the renowned Brooklyn Flea and Smorgasburg food fest at the river's edge.

## THE BASICS

**Brooklyn Heights**
✚ H22
🚇 2, 3 Clark Street
**Brooklyn Museum of Art**
brooklynmuseum.org
✚ See map ▷ 110
✉ 200 Eastern Parkway
☎ 718/638-5000
🕐 Wed, Fri–Sun 11–6, Thu 11–10
🚇 2, 3, Eastern Parkway–Brooklyn Museum
♿ Moderate
**Prospect Park**
✚ See map ▷ 110
☎ 718/965-8951
🚇 2, 3 Grand Army Plaza Station; F 15th Street–Prospect Park
**Williamsburg**
✚ See map ▷ 111
**Brooklyn Flea and Smorgasburg**
brooklynflea.com
✉ East River State Park, 50 Kent Street
🕐 Smorgasburg: Saturday; Brooklyn Flea: Sunday; check website for details
🚇 L Bedford Avenue
♿ Inexpensive

## HIGHLIGHTS

- Delacorte Theater, Shakespeare in the Park
- Summer stage concerts
- Conservatory Water
- Bethesda Fountain
- Wollman Rink in winter
- Heckscher Playground
- Swedish Cottage Marionette Theatre
- Walking in the Ramble

## TIPS

- Don't walk alone in isolated areas at night.
- Watch out for bicycles on the roads.

The park is the escape valve for the city. Without it New York would overheat—especially in summer, when the humidity tops 90 percent. Bikers, runners, dog walkers and frisbee players convene here. It's a way of life.

**The Greensward Plan** In the mid-19th century, when few lived in Manhattan north of 42nd Street, *New York Evening Post* editor William Cullen Bryant campaigned until the city invested $5 million in 843 acres (340ha) of undeveloped land. Responsible for clearing the land was journalist Frederick Law Olmsted, who, with English architect Calvert Vaux, also won the competition to design the park with his "Greensward Plan." Five million cubic tons of dirt were cleared to create this green space.

*Clockwise from left: The Pond, at the south end of Central Park; a bronze statue depicting characters in Lewis Carroll's* Alice in Wonderland, *just north of the Conservatory Water; Sheep Meadow, a great place to throw frisbees; the tribute to John Lennon in Strawberry Fields*

**Fun and games** Start at the Dairy Visitor Center and pick up a map and events list. These show the layout of the park and tell you about the Wildlife Conservation Center (Zoo), the Carousel, the playgrounds, rinks, fountains, statues and Strawberry Fields, where John Lennon is commemorated close to the Dakota Building, where he lived and was shot. But the busy life of the park is not recorded on maps: making music on the Mall; sunbathing in Sheep Meadow; hanging out at the Heckscher Playground and Great Lawn softball leagues; doing the loop road by bike; sailing toy boats on the Conservatory Water; bird-watching in the Ramble; jogging around the Reservoir; rowing on the Lake beneath the lovely Bow Bridge; fishing at Harlem Meer; or bouldering on the outcrops of Manhattan schist (rock).

**THE BASICS**

centralparknyc.org

D2–D9

212/310-6600

Dairy Visitor Center, 65th Street, daily 10–5; 3 other kiosks throughout park Apr–Nov only

Restaurants, kiosks

A, B, C, D, 1 59th Street–Columbus Circle; N, Q, R 57th Street–7th Avenue or 5th Avenue–59th Street, F 57th Street; 4, 5, 6 86th Street

M1, M2, M3, M4, M5, M10. Crosstown M66, M30, M72, M86

Moderate

Free

### HIGHLIGHTS

● Mahayana Buddhist
Temple (✉ 133 Canal
Street ◷ Daily 8.30–6
💰 Donation)
● Museum of Chinese in
America (▷ 70)
● New Kam Man (200
Canal Street, ▷ 124)
● Doyers Street
● Columbus Park
(✉ Bayard/Baxter streets)

### TIP

● Visit Columbus Park,
where you can see every-
thing from fortune tellers to
tai chi to Chinese singers
and instrumentalists, who
perform near the pavilion
on weekends.

New York's Chinatown has swallowed
nearly all of Little Italy and has spread over
a great deal of the Lower East Side. Wander
here and become immersed by the sights
and sounds of a busy Asian community.

**Going west** Chinese people first came to New
York in the late 19th century, fleeing persecu-
tion on the west coast. But, by 1880, some
10,000 men—mostly Cantonese railroad
workers—had settled among the Irish and
Italians of the old Five Points area. The Chinese
Exclusion Act (1883) kept the community small
until immigration restrictions were lifted in
1965. While the first arrivals were mostly
Cantonese speakers, most of today's immigrants are Fujianese. New York has two more
Chinatowns: in Flushing (Queens) and Eighth

*Clockwise from left: A colorful and vibrant area, Manhattan's Chinatown is a long-established Asian enclave and the largest Chinatown in the world; a quiet spot for a Chinese board game; a statue of Confucius; snakeskins for sale at a Chinese herbalist*

Avenue, Brooklyn, with thousands of residents. Manhattan's, though, is the largest in the western hemisphere.

**A closed world** Although Chinatown is welcoming to visitors, you may never penetrate its culture. Many of its denizens never learn English and never leave its environs. Many work in the neighborhood's restaurants, which range from hole-in-the-wall dumpling joints to old-fashioned Cantonese fare that harkens back to an earlier era. Catch a glimpse of this vibrant culture at the Mahayana Buddhist Temple, with its 16ft (4.8m) Buddha; in the markets that line Canal and Grand streets; or at the Museum of Chinese in America (▷ 70), which tells the story of New York's Chinese community from its inception to the present day.

**THE BASICS**

explorechinatown.com

➕ F19–20

✉ Roughly delineated by Worth Street/East Broadway, the Bowery, Grand Street, Centre Street

🍴 Numerous (some close around 10pm)

🚇 6, N, Q, R, J, Z Canal Street; B, D Grand Street

🚌 M22, M103

♿ Poor

❓ Visitors' Kiosk at Canal and Baxter streets, daily 10–6

# 5 Cooper Hewitt Smithsonian Design Museum

America's sole design museum is a marvelous showcase of everything from cutting-edge work by up-and-coming artists to classic examples of fine furnishings and accessories. All of it is housed in one of New York's most stunning mansions.

**Carnegie and Cooper and Hewitt** The mansion that contains this superb collection belonged to industrialist Andrew Carnegie, who, in 1903, had asked architects Babb, Cook & Willard for "the most modest, plainest and most roomy house in New York City." This he did not receive (aside from the roominess), since this little chateau was built with modern conveniences galore—air-conditioning and elevators—and a big gated garden. The entire neighborhood came to be known as Carnegie

Left: The entrance to the Cooper Hewitt Smithsonian Design Museum on East 91st Street; below: The Museum's Arthur Ross Terrace and Garden is often used to host art installations and events

Hill. Andrew's wife, Louise, lived here until her death in 1946. Twenty years later, the collection of the Hewitt sisters (decorative arts, ceramics, textiles, and more), which had been previously exhibited at the Cooper Union (▷ 24) became a part of the Smithsonian and moved into the mansion.

**State of the Art** The museum's 2014 revamp was designed to make its exhibitions more interactive. In the Immersion Room, you can project textile patterns onto blank walls and then create your own. In the Process Lab you can make your own protoype or see a 3D printer in action. However, these state-of-the-art exhibits have not displaced the Hewitt sisters' core collection and Carnegie's home is still shown to good effect.

## THE BASICS

cooperhewitt.org
✚ E4
✉ 2 E 91st Street
☎ 212/849-8400
🕐 Sun–Fri 10–6, Sat 10–9
🍴 Café
🚇 4, 5, 6 86th Street
🚌 M1, M2, M3, M4
♿ Good
✋ Expensive
❓ Free tours daily

### HIGHLIGHTS

● Merchant's House Museum
● Strolling St. Mark's Place
● Diverse array of foods

### TIP

● The Strand (▷ 125) on Broadway has 18 miles (29km) of shelves packed with new and used titles. In an area that was once lined with second-hand book-shops, the Strand is one of the few remaining places to find obscure titles.

Once an immigrant neighborhood—and then the rundown bohemia celebrated in the musical *Rent*—the East Village is now prime real estate. Nearby NoHo is quieter and full of historic streets and sites.

**Early days** What was once Dutch Governor Peter Stuyvesant's farm, or bowery, later became a mostly German enclave. Jews, Poles, and Ukrainians followed. Meanwhile, streets such as Bond and Lafayette in what is today the section called NoHo (North of Houston) were home to New York's mercantile elite, including John Jacob Astor, the country's richest man.

**Historic sites** Cooper Union, founded by industrialist Peter Cooper and built in 1859, was the spot where Abraham Lincoln gave his

*Clockwise from far left: Cooper Union, an East Village landmark; trading on the area's literary associations; the neighborhood's Ukrainian heritage is celebrated at the Ukrainian Museum; architectural detail inside Grace Church; an East Village mural*

landmark "Right Makes Might" anti-slavery speech. The city's second-oldest church, St. Mark's Church-in-the-Bowery, boasts Peter Stuyvesant's grave. On Broadway, Grace Church (▷ 68) was the debut of architect James Renwick, who went on to build St. Patrick's Cathedral (▷ 71). The Ukrainian Museum, in the heart of the immigrant neighborhood, features textiles and beautifully decorated Easter eggs. In NoHo, the Merchant's House Museum is an intact early 19th-century home lived in by the same family for nearly a century.

**St. Mark's Place** The main thoroughfare of the East Village is St. Mark's. In the 1960s, counter-culture exploded along this street, which included Andy Warhol's Electric Circus. Today it is a mix of shops, restaurants and tattoo parlors.

## THE BASICS

➕ F16; east of Broadway and south of 14th Street

🚇 F, M Lower East Side-2nd Avenue; 6 Astor Place

**Ukrainian Museum**

ukrainianmuseum.org

➕ F17

✉ 222 E 6th Street/2nd–3rd avenues

☎ 212/228-0110

🕐 Wed–Sun 11.30–5

♿ Good 💲 Moderate

**Merchant's House Museum**

merchantshouse.org

➕ E17

✉ 29 E 4th Street/Lafayette–Bowery

☎ 212/777-1089

🕐 Thu 12–8, Fri–Mon 12–5

♿ Poor 💲 Moderate

## HIGHLIGHTS

● Wall of Honor
● Peopling of America galleries
● The American Flag of Faces™

## TIP

● To avoid lines and wait times, try to be on the first ferry to Ellis Island (which also serves the Statue of Liberty). The lines and wait times to board ferries grow exponentially during the day, especially in summer.

Visiting Ellis Island, the gateway to America for millions of immigrants from 1892–1954, is a poignant reminder of the obstacles so many people had to overcome to reach this country.

**Half of all America**  It was the poor immigrants who docked at Ellis Island, since travelers in first-class passage were given permission to disembark straight into Manhattan. Young Annie Moore, aged 15 and the first immigrant to land at Ellis Island, arrived in 1892. She was followed by some 16 million immigrants over the next 40 years, including such future success stories as Irving Berlin and Frank Capra. Unsurprisingly, around one-third of the current population of the United States can trace their roots to an Ellis Island immigrant.

*Clockwise from far left: Exhibition documenting the arrival of early immigrants to New York; statue of Annie Moore, the first immigrant to arrive at Ellis Island; the Great Hall; view of Ellis Island from the ferry; the view of Lower Manhattan from Ellis Island; an immigrant's records*

**Island of Hope, Island of Tears** The exhibition in the main building conveys the indignities, frustrations and fears of the immigrants. Choose a ranger-guided tour or the free, 45-minute audio tour which accompanies you around the route that new arrivals took, from the Baggage Room, where people had to abandon all they owned, then onward to the Registry Room and through the inspection chambers, where the medical, mental and political status of each immigrant was ascertained. In the museum, the American Family Immigration History Center® gives access to passenger ship records of millions of immigrants (for a fee). The Peopling of America galleries tell of the hardships and struggles of immigrants in the years preceding and post the island's processing station.

### THE BASICS

nps.gov/elis

🔲 See map ▷ 110

✉ Ellis Island

☎ 212/363–3200

🕐 Daily 9.30–5; extended hours in summer

🍴 Café

🚇 4, 5 Bowling Green, 1 South Ferry, then take ferry

🚌 M5, M20, M15 South Ferry, then take the ferry

⛴ Ferry departs Battery Park South Ferry every 30 min. Ferry information tel 877/523-9849, statuecruises.com

♿ Good

🎫 Museum free; ferry expensive

❓ Audio tours

# 8 Empire State Building

## HIGHLIGHTS

● The view at any time of day or night
● The view up from 34th Street
● Observatory Audio Tour
● Marble art deco lobby

## TIPS

● Avoid the line (though not the security check) by printing out advance tickets from the website.
● The colored lights at the summit were introduced in 1976 and are changed to mark different events.

Though it lost its crown as world's tallest building more than four decades ago, the Empire State Building remains New York's most famous skyscraper. Known around the world from movies such as *King Kong*, *An Affair to Remember* and *Sleepless in Seattle*, the 86th-floor Observatory is worth the long lines.

**King for 40 years** This is the very definition of "skyscraper," and it was the highest in America until the late, lamented World Trade Center was built in the 1970s. Now it has once again been overtaken as the tallest building in New York, this time by One World Trade Center.

Construction began in 1930, not long after the great Wall Street Crash. By the time it was topped out in 1931—construction went at the

Left: Head to the Observatory on the 86th floor for panoramic views of New York; below: There are good views of the Empire State Building itself from 34th Street

superfast rate of four stories a week—few could afford to rent space, and they called it the "Empty State Building." Only the popularity of its observatories kept the wolves from the door. These views still attract up to four million visitors each year. The open-air 86th floor Observatory is a highlight.

**The facts** It is 1,454ft (443m) high, with 103 floors. The frame contains 60,000 tons of steel, 10 million bricks line the building, and there are 6,500 windows. The speediest elevator climbs about 1,000ft (330m) per minute. The fastest runners in the annual Empire State Run-Up climb the 1,860 steps (not open to the public) to the 102nd floor in just over nine minutes. The observation deck on the 102nd floor requires a separate ticket and additional fee.

## THE BASICS

esbnyc.com

➕ E13

✉ 350 5th Avenue/ W 34th Street

☎ 212/736-3100

🕐 Daily 8am–2am; last admission 1.15am

🍴 Restaurants

Ⓑ B, D, F, N, Q, R 34th Street–Herald Square

🚌 M1, M2, M3, M4, M5

🚉 PATH 34th Street–Avenue of the Americas

♿ Good

💲 Expensive

## HIGHLIGHTS

- Shopping!
- Empire State Building
- Rockefeller Center
- The Met
- The Guggenheim
- Cooper Hewitt

## TIP

- Try to see a parade—
St. Patrick's Day Parade, the
biggest, is on March 17.

Fifth Avenue is still the grand old dame of New York shopping, its Midtown section lined with prestigious stores. There's a lot more to see along this 6-mile (10km) thoroughfare though—famous museums, historic mansions and glorious Central Park.

**Tradition and invention** Fifth Avenue runs all the way from Washington Square Park up past Central Park and houses some of the most pricey and notable real estate in New York. Walk along the avenue and you'll pass the Flatiron Building (▷ 68), the Empire State Building (▷ 28–29), the New York Public Library (▷ 48–49), Rockefeller Center (▷ 50–51), St. Patrick's Cathedral (▷ 71), the Frick Collection (▷ 32–33), the Metropolitan Museum of Art (▷ 44–45), the Guggenheim

*Clockwise from far left: For most visitors Fifth Avenue is synonymous with shopping; Saks Fifth Avenue, one of New York's most prestigious department stores; designer brands abound; the Apple Store, a 24-hour temple of technology*

(▷ 38–39), and the Cooper Hewitt Smithsonian Design Museum (▷ 22–23), just a few of the buildings that represent the development of Fifth Avenue.

**Shop, shop, shop** Stores along Fifth are generally high end, but window shopping is encouraged. Start with the jewelry emporia of Tiffany & Co. (57th Street) and Cartier (No. 653), the 24-hour Apple Store (▷ 119) or the department stores. Saks Fifth Avenue (▷ 125) has been here since 1922. Bergdorf Goodman (▷ 120) is at 58th Street, and the fashion focus Henri Bendel is at 56th, along with Abercrombie & Fitch. If you plan to shop till you drop, two excellent hotels stand opposite each other on Fifth Avenue and 55th Street: the Peninsula New York and the St. Regis (▷ 158).

## THE BASICS

➕ E16–E7

✉ From Washington Square to the Harlem River

🚇 4, 5, 6 (various stops), R 5th Avenue–59th Street, E, M 5th Avenue–53rd Street

🚌 M1, M2, M3, M4

## HIGHLIGHTS

- *St. Jerome*, El Greco (c.1590–1600)
- *Sir Thomas More*, Holbein (1527)
- *Officer and the Laughing Girl*, Vermeer (c.1657)
- *The Polish Rider*, Rembrandt (c.1655)
- *The Progress of Love*, Fragonard (1771–72)
- *Philip IV of Spain*, Velázquez (1644)

To step inside Henry Clay Frick's magnificent Beaux Arts mansion on Fifth Avenue is half the reason for coming here. Henry Frick bequeathed his riches to the nation as a memorial to himself—that's the kind of guy he was.

**The man and the mansion**  Henry Clay Frick (1849–1919) was chairman of the Carnegie Steel Corp. He was a ruthless strike-breaker and one of the nastiest industrialists of his day. Instead of receiving any comeuppance (though there were assassination attempts), he got to commission Carrère and Hastings to build him one of the last great Beaux Arts mansions on Fifth Avenue and filled it with an exquisite collection of 14th- to 19th-century paintings, porcelain, furniture and bronzes.

Left: The oak-paneled Living Hall in the center of the mansion displays works by Holbein, El Greco, Titian and Bellini; below: The Fifth Avenue Garden

**What Frick bought** Some of the 40 rooms are arranged around a particular work or artist, notably the Boucher Room, east of the entrance, and the Fragonard Room, with the *Progress of Love* series. There are British (Constable, Gainsborough, Whistler, Turner), Dutch (Vermeer, Rembrandt, Van Eyck, Hals), Italian (Titian, Bellini, Veronese) and Spanish (El Greco, Goya, Velázquez) masters. Alongside the paintings are Limoges enamel and Chinese porcelain, Persian carpets and Marie Antoinette's furniture. You can admire a Louis XVI chair before strolling through the central glass-roofed courtyard. The Fifth Avenue Garden is a delight also.

Much of the mansion remains off-view to visitors, including the second-floor private apartments and a bowling alley in the basement.

| THE BASICS |
| --- |
| frick.org |
| ✚ E7 |
| ✉ 1 E 70th Street |
| ☎ 212/288-0700 |
| ◷ Tue–Sat 10–6, Sun 11–5 |
| Ⓡ 6 68th Street–Hunter College |
| 🚌 M1, M2, M3, M4 |
| ♿ Good |
| 💷 Expensive |
| ❓ Audio tours; for concerts, lectures and docent talks see calendar |

### HIGHLIGHTS

● Main concourse ceiling
● Oyster Bar
● Chandeliers
● Whispering Gallery
● The clock
● The 75ft (23m) arched windows
● Grand Staircase
● The Dining Concourse (▷ 145)
● The Campbell Apartment cocktail bar

### TIP

● After admiring the building, visit the many boutiques, gourmet market, and the annex of the New York Transit Museum.

Officially called Grand Central Terminal because the tracks all terminate here, this Beaux Arts masterpiece is not only an architectural marvel but one of the biggest stations in the world.

**Heart of the nation** "Grand Central Station!" bellowed (erroneously) the 1937 opening of the eponymous NBC radio drama; "Beneath the glitter and swank of Park Avenue… Crossroads of a million private lives!…Heart of the nation's greatest city…" And so it is, and has been since 1871, when the first, undersize version of the station was opened by Commodore Cornelius Vanderbilt, who had bought up all the city's railroads. See him in bronze below Jules-Alexis Coutan's allegorical statuary on the main facade (south, 42nd

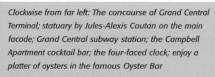

*Clockwise from far left: The concourse of Grand Central Terminal; statuary by Jules-Alexis Coutan on the main facade; Grand Central subway station; the Campbell Apartment cocktail bar; the four-faced clock; enjoy a platter of oysters in the famous Oyster Bar*

Street). The current building dates from 1913 and is another Beaux Arts glory, its design modeled partly on the Paris Opéra by the architectural firm Warren and Wetmore.

**Look within** Inside, the main concourse soars 12 stories high, with gleaming gold chandeliers and grand marble staircases at either end. Be careful what you say here—the acoustics are amazing. Look up at the ceiling for the stunning sight of 2,500 "stars" in an azure sky, with zodiac signs by French artist Paul Helleu. The fame of the brass clock with its four opalescent glass faces atop the information booth is out of proportion to its size. Below ground is a warren of 32 miles (52km) of tracks, tunnels and chambers; in one the famed Oyster Bar & Restaurant resides.

## THE BASICS

grandcentralterminal.com
✚ E11
✉ E 42nd Street/Park Avenue
☎ 212/340-2583
🕐 Daily 5.30am–2am
🍴 Restaurant, café/bar, snack bars 🚇 4, 5, 6, 7, S Grand Central–42nd Street
🚌 M1, M2, M3, M4, M42, M101, M102, M103 Grand Central 🚆 Metro North, Grand Central
♿ Good 🎟 Free
❓ Both self-guided audio tours (moderate; daily 9–6) and the guided Municipal Art Society tours (expensive; daily 12.30pm) leave from the GCT Tour windows on the main concourse

### HIGHLIGHTS

- Charming boutiques
- Washington Square Park
- NYC's narrowest house (75½ Bedford Street)
- Christopher Park
- Halloween parade
- Jefferson Market Library
- Italian restaurants on Bleecker Street
- MacDougal Street

### TIP

- Bleecker Street, one of the main drags through the Village, is lined with one-of-a-kind stores, music bars and great pizza parlors.

The Village (never just "Greenwich") has long been a bohemian mecca, and its picturesque neighborhoods, lined with trees and brownstones, form a romantic image of Manhattan.

**Artists, writers, musicians** First settled by the Dutch as Noortwijck, the Village became a refuge in the 18th and early 19th centuries for wealthy New Yorkers escaping epidemics in the city. When the elite moved on, the bohemian invasion began. Edgar Allan Poe moved to West Third Street in 1845. Fellow literary habitués included Mark Twain, O. Henry, Walt Whitman, F. Scott Fitzgerald and Eugene O'Neill. After World War II, artists Jackson Pollock, Mark Rothko and Willem de Kooning also lived here. Bob Dylan made his name in Village music

*Clockwise from far left: Bars and restaurants abound in the Village; detail of the Gay Liberation Monument in Christopher Park; Bleecker Street has many restaurants; Christopher Street has great shops; getting around in the Village; desirable St. Luke's Place*

clubs in the 1960s, while the Blue Note (▷ 132) and Village Vanguard clubs remain hotbeds of jazz today.

**Freedom parades** When police raided the Stonewall Inn on June 28, 1969, and arrested gay men for illegally buying drinks, they set off the Stonewall Riots—the birth of the Gay Rights movement. The Inn is on Christopher Street, which became the center of New York's gay community. Statues of gay and lesbian couples stand in tiny Christopher Park. The Washington Memorial Arch (▷ 73) towers over Washington Square Park, a lively hangout for university students. As you explore, look out for the ornate Jefferson Market Library (6th Avenue and W 10th Street), the quaint Cherry Lane Theatre on Commerce Street, and tiny Minetta Lane.

### THE BASICS

➕ C17–D17

✉ East–west from Broadway to Hudson Street; north–south from 14th Street to Houston Street

🍴 Numerous

🚇 A, B, C, D, E, F 4th Street–Washington Square; 1 Christopher Street–Sheridan Square

🚌 M5

🚉 PATH Christopher Street

♿ Poor

## HIGHLIGHTS

- The building
- *L'Hermitage à Pontoise*, Pissarro (1867)
- *Paris Through the Window*, Chagall (1913)
- *Woman Ironing*, Picasso (1904)
- *Nude*, Modigliani (1917)
- Kandinskys
- Klees
- Légers
- The store

### TIP

- Museum admission is pay-what-you-wish on Saturdays 5.45–7.45, but get there early as lines can be long.

Now considered one of his masterpieces, Frank Lloyd Wright's spiral-shaped museum building was originally derided by critics, who compared it to a jello mold.

**Museum of architecture** This is the great architect's only major New York building. It was commissioned by Solomon R. Guggenheim at the urging of his friend and taste tutor Baroness Hilla von Rebay though, unfortunately, the wealthy metal-mining magnate died 10 years before it was completed in 1959.

The giant white nautilus is certainly arresting, but it's the interior that unleashes the most superlatives. Take the elevator to the top level and snake your way down the museum's spiral ramp to experience the full effects of the building's design. You can study the exhibits (albeit

Left: The spiral walkway inside the Guggenheim Museum;
below: The Guggenheim's curvy exterior

in reverse order), look over the parapet to the
lobby below, and finish up where you began.

**Museum of art** There are some 6,000 pieces
in the Guggenheim Foundation's possession.
Solomon and his wife Irene Rothschild
abandoned collecting old masters when
Hilla von Rebay introduced them to Léger,
Kandinsky, Chagall, Mondrian, Moholy-Nagy
and Gleizes, and they became hooked on the
moderns. See early Picassos in the small
rotunda and the tower extension. For
Impressionists and Postimpressionists, look
for the Thannhauser Collection, always on display—unlike the rotated Guggenheim holdings,
which are shown in themed exhibitions. The
museum continues to acquire works, including
pieces by Matthew Barney and Agathe Snow.

## THE BASICS

guggenheim.org

✚ E5

✉ 1071 5th Avenue/
89th Street

☎ 212/423-3500

🕐 Sun–Wed, Fri 10–5.45,
Sat 10–7.45

🍴 Café

Ⓢ 4, 5, 6 86th Street

🚌 M1, M2, M3, M4

♿ Good

💵 Expensive

❓ Lecture program;
audio tours

- The Whitney Museum
- Site-specific art installations
- Northern spur preserve
- 10th Avenue Square

**TIP**

- Because the park keeps entirely to the original rail line, narrow sections can be crowded. Come early before the day heats up or enjoy a leisurely stroll just before sunset.

Today this beautiful elevated park attracts more annual visitors than the Statue of Liberty. Yet just a decade ago, the High Line was a weed-choked, abandoned rail line snaking through the industrial waterfront.

**Train tracks** Manhattan in the 19th-century was the largest port in America, with many commercial piers lining the Hudson River. To move the huge amount of goods, Tenth Avenue was overlaid with railroad tracks so dangerous that the street was nicknamed Death Avenue. In the early 1930s, the trains were moved to a second-story elevated track running through many of the factories and warehouses, including the giant Nabisco headquarters (birthplace of the Oreo cookie) that is now Chelsea Market (▷ 121).

Far left: View of New York's High Line Park, running under the Standard Hotel between 12th and 13th streets; Below: Planting on the High Line incorporates many hardy and perennial species that could once be found growing alongside the original rail tracks

**Friends of the High Line** After the freight line folded, the abandoned sections of track became overgrown. In 1999, Friends of the High Line formed to advocate turning this wilderness into an amenity. A park was opened and now stretches 1.45 miles (2.3km) from Gansevoort Street to West 34th Street. The park's popularity has been a boon for the surrounding neighborhood, drawing new luxury condos, hotels (like the Standard, which straddles the park) and restaurants to the area. Where the tracks cross 10th Avenue at 17th Street, seating allows visitors to gaze uptown; a few steps south, an overgrown spur track recalls what the High Line looked like before renovation work. In summer, the park hosts temporary exhibitions, and the park's southern end joins the new home of the Whitney Museum of American Art (▷ 60–61).

## THE BASICS

thehighline.org
✚ A13, B13–16
✉ Gansevoort Street to W 34th Street between 10th and 12th avenues (staircases up to the park located every 2–3 blocks)
☎ 212/206-9922
🕐 Daily Jun–Sep 7am–11pm; Apr–May, Oct–Nov 7am–10pm; Dec–Mar 7–7
🍴 Numerous
🚇 A, C, E 14th Street; L 8th Avenue; 7 34th Street–Hudson Yards
🚌 M11, M12, M14, M23, M34
🎟 Free

### HIGHLIGHTS

● Chandeliers in the Met foyer and auditorium
● Reflecting Pool with Henry Moore's *Reclining Figure* (1965)
● Lincoln Center Out-of-Doors Festival in summer
● NY City Ballet's *Nutcracker* in December
● Chagall murals in the foyer of the Met
● Free concerts at the David Rubenstein Atrium
● New York Film Festival
● The Revson Fountain in the Central Plaza
● Jazz at Lincoln Center
● Annual *Messiah* singalong

### TIP

● Dance under the stars at the Midsummer Night's Swing in Josie Robertson Plaza, a summertime series of live band sessions.

Strolling across the Central Plaza to the fantastically lit 10-story colonnade of the Metropolitan Opera House on a deep winter's night is one of the most glamorous things you can do in this city, and you don't need tickets to come and look.

*West Side Story* The Rockefeller-funded arts center was envisaged in the late 1950s and finished in 1969, after 7,000 families and 800 businesses had been pushed aside by city planner Robert Moses. The opening scene of *West Side Story* was filmed here after the demolition began.

**All the arts** The 16-acre (6ha) site includes several of New York's top arts venues, all designed by different architects in the same

*Clockwise from left: The Revson Fountain, between the David H. Koch Theater (left) and the Metropolitan Opera House (right); the David Rubenstein Atrium is a great place to meet up with friends; Alice Tully Hall, one of several classical music venues; visitors to the Lincoln Center*

white travertine. The Metropolitan Opera House is the glamor queen, with her vast Marc Chagall murals, red carpet, fabulous sweeping staircase and sparkling chandeliers that thrillingly rise to the gold-leaf ceiling before performances. You can take a fascinating backstage tour. David Geffen Hall is home to America's oldest orchestra, the NY Philharmonic, while the Juilliard School of Music supplies the ensemble with fresh talent. The David H. Koch Theater, housing the New York City Ballet, faces David Geffen Hall across the Plaza. The Franklin P. Rose Hall is the centerpiece of Jazz at Lincoln Center in the Time Warner Center down the street. A Broadway house, two smaller theaters, and a more intimate concert hall, Alice Tully, plus the Walter Reade movie theater and many smaller venues, complete the pack.

## THE BASICS

lincolncenter.org

➕ B8

✉ 64th Street at Columbus Avenue

☎ Met 212/362-6000, David Geffen Hall 212/875-5030, Jazz 212/721-6500

🕐 Inquire for performance times

🍴 Restaurants, cafés, bars

🚇 1 66th Street–Lincoln Center

🚌 M5, M7, M10, M11, M104, M66

♿ Good

🎫 Center admission free

❓ Tours daily from David Rubenstein Atrium, tel 212/875-5350

43

## HIGHLIGHTS

- Temple of Dendur (15BC)
- Period rooms, American Wing
- 19th- and early 20th-century art galleries
- Decorative arts from the Far East
- Greco-Roman galleries

## TIP

- On Friday and Saturday evenings when the museum stays open late, enjoy a cocktail and live music on the mezzanine.

The third largest art museum in the world (after the Louvre and the Hermitage) has something for everyone, from ancient artifacts to arms and armor, cutting-edge fashion and some of the most famous paintings in the world.

**Art history 101** The Met's collection is renowned for its stunning breadth and depth. In fact, the museum is so huge that visitors are advised to either do a whirlwind tour (with or without a museum guide) or choose one period or area to explore in depth, whether that's ancient Greece, Africa or the summer rooftop installations.

**Buildings upon buildings** The Met is housed in three separate locations: the main museum

*Clockwise from left: The Met's European Sculpture Court; Wheat Field with Cypresses, Vincent van Gogh (1889), the European Paintings and Sculpture Room; the Beaux Arts facade of the museum*

on Fifth Avenue, the Cloisters in Upper Manhattan (▷ 74) and the Met Breuer (▷ 69), a few minutes away on Madison Avenue. There are even more structures to be discovered inside the main headquarters, including the Egyptian temple of Dendur, the Astor Court (a Ming dynasty courtyard) in the Chinese galleries, a bank facade in the American wing, and the beautifully decorated Damascus room in the Islamic collection.

**Special exhibitions and more** The museum hosts homegrown and traveling exhibitions (included in the admission fee) along with concerts, lectures, gallery talks and site-specific music and dance events (for an extra charge). Check the museum's website in advance for these, as many special events sell out quickly.

## THE BASICS

metmuseum.org
✚ D5–6
✉ 1000 5th Avenue/82nd Street
☎ 212/535-7710
🕐 Sun–Thu 10–5.30, Fri–Sat 10–9
🍴 Cafeteria, restaurant, bar
🚇 4, 5, 6 86th Street
🚌 M1, M2, M3, M4
♿ Good
👐 Expensive
❓ Free guided tours leave from the information desk in the main lobby throughout the day

## HIGHLIGHTS

- *Hope*, Klimt (1907–08)
- *Dance*, Matisse (1909)
- *Les Demoiselles d'Avignon*, Picasso (1907)
- *Starry Night*, Van Gogh (1889)
- *Gas*, Hopper (1940)
- *One: Number 31*, Pollock (1950)
- *Flag*, Jasper Johns (1954–55)
- Sculpture Garden

Yoshio Taniguchi's MoMA expansion in 2004 doubled the museum's gallery space; now, the museum is poised to grow again, providing more room to showcase its unmatched collection of everything from Postimpressionist paintings to film.

**Postimpressionists to graffiti artists** Founded on the 1931 bequest of Lillie P. Bliss, which comprised 235 works of art, MoMA's collections now amount to about 150,000 pieces. These include household objects, photography, graphic design, conceptual art, industrial design and media. The collection starts in the late 19th century, with the Postimpressionists and later Fauvists. Among the 20th-century movements represented in the museum are Cubism, Futurism, Expressionism, Surrealism, Abstract

Left: Gallery with Wilhelm Lehmbruck's Standing Youth to the fore and paintings by Chagall (left of the statue) and František Kupka (to the right); below: The stunning glass exterior of the MoMA, designed by the renowned Japanese architect Yoshio Taniguchi

Expressionism, Pop (Oldenburg, Dine, Rauschenberg and Warhol) and the "Graffiti" work of Keith Haring and Jean-Michel Basquiat.

**Even more modern** A sunlit, 110ft (33m) high atrium affords a view of the Abby Aldrich Rockefeller Sculpture Garden, a museum favorite containing such works as Picasso's *She-Goat* (1950) and Barnett Newman's *Broken Obelisk* (1963–69). The Sculpture Garden is open free of charge daily (9.30–10.15am), except in inclement weather. Taniguchi's building makes much use of glass, granite, aluminum and light, and individual galleries have been designed specifically for the media they house. Audio tours in multiple languages are available for download to your smartphone.

## THE BASICS

moma.org

🔂 D10

✉ 11 W 53rd Street/ 5th–6th avenues

☎ 212/708-9400

🕐 Sat–Thu 10.30–5.30, Fri 10.30–8

🍽 Restaurant

🚇 E, M 5th Avenue–53rd Street; B, D, F 47th–50th streets–Rockefeller Center

🚌 M1, 2, 3, 4, 5, 7

♿ Good

💲 Expensive; free Fri 4–8

## HIGHLIGHTS

● Patience and Fortitude
● Main Reading Room
● Thomas Jefferson's handwritten Declaration of Independence
● Astor Hall
● American Jewish Oral History Collection
● Gottesman Hall ceiling

## TIP

● It's worth taking one of the free one-hour tours (Mon–Sat 11, 2). Meet at the reception desk in Astor Hall.

The New York Public Library's Central Research Building is a great white, hushed palace, beautiful to behold even if you have no time to open any of its books. It is a US National Historic Landmark.

**The building** Along with the US Custom House (▷ 73) and Grand Central (▷ 34–35), this masterpiece by Carrère and Hastings is ranked as one of the best Beaux Arts buildings in New York and is a highlight of what was known as the City Beautiful era. In 2011 the library was discreetly rechristened the Stephen A. Schwarzman Building, after the Wall Street financier who donated $100 million towards its renovation. A pair of lions, named Patience and Fortitude by Mayor LaGuardia during the Depression, flank the stair that leads into the

Clockwise from far left: The Main Reading Room of the New York Public Library; Astor Hall, the starting point of guided tours; the exterior of the library, one of the finest Beaux Arts buildings in New York

white marble Astor Hall. Inside, see temporary exhibitions in the Gottesman Hall, and look skywards: The carved oak ceiling is sublime. Priceless items from the library's collection, such as the first Gutenberg Bible brought to the New World, line the balcony corridor or are displayed in upstairs rooms. Don't miss the stunning two-block-long reading rooms, or the Richard Haas murals of NYC publishing houses in the De Witt Wallace Periodical Room.

**The books** The library owns more than 18 million books, most of which are kept in the 91 branches. The 92 miles (148km) of holdings are solely for research. Books kept on the premises are sent to the reading room by dumbwaiter; for material kept offsite, researchers must make an appointment.

## THE BASICS

nypl.org

✚ E12

✉ 476 5th Avenue/ 42nd Street

☎ 917/275-6975

🕐 Mon, Thu–Sat 10–6, Tue–Wed 10–8, Sun 1–5

🍴 Kiosks outside (summer)

🚇 4, 5, 6, S Grand Central–42nd Street, 7 5th Avenue

🚌 M1, M2, M3, M4, M5, M7, M42

🚆 Metro North, Grand Central

♿ Good

👊 Free

# ★19 Rockefeller Center

**HIGHLIGHTS**

● Top of the Rock
Observation Deck
● 30 Rock's lobbies and the
Lee Lawrie friezes
● NBC Studio tour
● Skating in winter
● Radio City Music Hall
● *Prometheus* (1934)
● *Atlas* (5th Avenue,
50th–51st streets)

**TIP**

● There's a vast array of
shops, casual restaurants,
and more in a basement
arcade below the center.
There's a great vantage for
watching winter skaters
down there, too.

This complex of art deco buildings provides
many of those "Gee, this is New York"
moments, especially at Christmas when you
can watch ice-skaters ringed by the flags of
the UN and gaze up at the massive tree.

***Prometheus* is here** The 19-building
Rockefeller Center has been called the greatest
urban complex of the 20th century. John D.
Rockefeller Jr.'s grand real estate scheme pro-
vided work for 40,000 people during the
Depression. Its centerpiece is the elongated
ziggurat at 30 Rockefeller Plaza (officially now
the Comcast Building, formerly the GE
Building), adorned with Lee Lawrie's glass-and-
limestone frieze, lobby murals by José Maria
Sert and various other artworks. Rest for a while
on a Channel Gardens bench and gaze on the

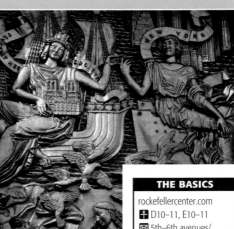

*Clockwise from far left: Radio City Music Hall forms part of Rockefeller Center; Paul Manship's bronze* Prometheus *(1934) on the Lower Plaza;* Friendship Between America and France *(1934), a gilded bronze by Alfred Janniot above the Fifth Avenue entrance*

Lower Plaza, the ice rink and Paul Manship's gilded bronze *Prometheus* (1934).

**Top of the Rock** The three-tiered observation deck on the 70th floor of 30 Rock affords stunning panoramic views over Manhattan and the only public overview of Central Park. The mezzanine museum tells the history of the complex before high-speed elevators whisk you to the 67th–70th floor viewing platforms.

**NBC and Rockettes** This is also the home of NBC Studios. Tours are led daily, or try for standby tickets to *Saturday Night Live* or one of the late-night talk shows filmed here. At Christmas time (and now in summer), the Rockettes hold court at Radio City Music Hall, the grandest theater in town.

## THE BASICS

rockefellercenter.com
✚ D10–11, E10–11
✉ 5th–6th avenues/48th–51st streets
☎ 212/588-8601
🕐 Various
🍴 Many restaurants, cafés
🚇 B, D, F, M 47th–50th streets–Rockefeller Center
🚌 M1, M2, M3, M4, M5, M7, M50
♿ Moderate
🎟 Free
❓ Radio City tours, tel 212/247-4777; NBC Studio tours, tel 212/664-3700; Rockefeller Center tours, tel 212/698-2000

**Top of the Rock**
topoftherocknyc.com
☎ 212/698-2000
🕐 Daily 8am–midnight (last elevator 11pm)
🎟 Expensive

## HIGHLIGHTS

- Shopping
- King and Queen of Greene Street
- Little Singer Building
- Haughwout Building

## TIP

- Stop at Dean & DeLuca (Broadway and Prince) for a coffee and pastry, a hot sandwich or to browse its delectable gourmet fare, including its cheese and dessert counters.

In the last 150 years, SoHo has come full circle. New York's smartest shopping district around the time of the Civil War, the area fell on hard times by World War II. Now, its landmark cast-iron buildings teem with trendy shops again.

**Cast in iron** An acronym for "South of Houston," SoHo stretches for several delightful blocks between Houston and Canal streets, bordered by Lafayette Street on the east and Sixth Avenue to the west. Around 500 of its 19th-century industrial buildings have been preserved in the SoHo Cast Iron Historic District. Inexpensive, strong and easy to mold, cast iron made it possible to erect ornate buildings in Italianate and other elaborate styles quickly and cheaply. Some of the finest examples are

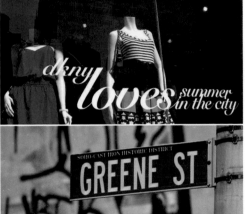

*Clockwise from far left: The Little Singer Building in the SoHo Cast Iron Historic District; sculpture inspired by the well-known 1932 photograph of New York ironworkers eating lunch while sitting on a girder; fashion stores; a great place to stroll; art galleries abound*

the King (No. 72) and Queen (No. 28) of Greene Street, the Little Singer Building (561 Broadway) and the Haughwout Building (488 Broadway), which had the first Otis steam passenger elevator. Old-fashioned lampposts further enhance SoHo's charm.

**Art and fashion** By the 1960s and 70s, many of SoHo's commercial buildings were abandoned. Then, artists moved in, art galleries followed, and SoHo became the most fashionable quarter in town. Rising prices forced many artists and galleries to Chelsea and beyond, but fashionistas quickly filled the empty and spacious showrooms. Everything from Prada's flagship store to branches of Bloomingdale's and London's Topshop to designer boutiques make this a shopper's heaven.

## THE BASICS

➕ E18–19

✉ Houston–Canal streets, Lafayette Street–6th Avenue

🍴 Numerous

🚇 N, R Prince Street; 6 Spring Street; C, E Spring Street

🚌 M5, M21

♿ Moderate

### HIGHLIGHTS

● View from the crown
● Statue of Liberty Museum, including the original torch
● Fort Wood, the star-shaped pedestal base

### TIP

● Visits to the crown must be reserved well in advance (sometimes months) on tel 201/604-2800 or online at statuecruises.com. There are no same-day crown tickets available.

Liberty Enlightening the World (as she's formally known), famous symbol of the American dream of freedom, takes your breath away, however many times you've seen her image.

**How she grew** In the late 1860s, sculptor Frédéric-Auguste Bartholdi dreamed of placing a monument to freedom in a prominent location. His dream merged with the French historian Edouard-René de Laboulaye's idea of presenting the American people with a statue that celebrated freedom and the two nations' friendship. Part of the idea was to shame the repressive French government but, apparently, New Yorkers took their freedom for granted. It was only after Joseph Pulitzer promised to print the name of every donor in his newspaper, the

*Clockwise from far left: Liberty Island, a beacon of hope since 1886; Liberty's seven-pointed crown; the symbol of American liberty raises her torch to the world*

*New York World*, that citizens coughed up the funds to build the pedestal. Liberty was unveiled by President Grover Cleveland on October 28, 1886.

**Mother of exiles** Beneath her 25ft-long (8m) feet, she tramples the shackles of tyranny, and her seven-pointed crown beams liberty to the seven continents and the seven seas. Gustave Eiffel designed the 1,700-bar iron and steel structure that supports her. She weighs 225 tons, is 151ft (46m) tall, and is covered in 300 copper plates. The tablet she holds reads: July IV MDCCLXXVI—the date of the Declaration of Independence. The torch tip towers 305ft (93m) above sea level. In the museum in the statue's base you can read Emma Lazarus's stirring poem *The New Colossus*.

## THE BASICS

nps.gov/stli
➕ See map ▷ 110
✉ Liberty Island
☎ 212/363-3200
🕐 Daily 9.30–5; extended hours in peak season. A limited number of daily tickets to tour the pedestal/museum may be reserved in advance from ferry office, by phone or online
🍴 Cafeteria
🚇 4, 5 Bowling Green, 1 South Ferry, then take ferry
🚌 M5, M15, M20 South Ferry, then take ferry
⛴ Departs Battery Park
☎ 877/523-9849; statuecruises.com
♿ Poor
🎟 Free; ferry expensive

55

### HIGHLIGHTS

- Neon lights at night
- Shubert Alley
- 42nd Street
- ABC's *Good Morning* studio: 44th/Broadway
- New Year's Eve ball drop

### TIP

- The TKTS booth, located at Duffy Square, 47th Street/Broadway, sells same-day theater tickets for 20–50 percent off. The booth is open daily 3–8 for evening shows (from 2pm Tue), Wed, Thu and Sat 10–2 for matinees, Sun 11–7 for all shows.

"The Crossroads of the World," one-time symbol of Manhattan glitz and glam, is bright, bold and exciting—there is always something going on here. Beneath the dazzling neon signs big-name stores and entertainment venues do a brisk trade.

**Longacre Square** The junction of Broadway and Seventh Avenue was called Longacre Square until the Times Tower, the new home of the *New York Times*, was finished in 1904. Almost immediately, the relocation of the theater district, the opening of the first subway and the decision to site the New Year celebration here made it the de facto center of Manhattan.

**On Broadway** The theaters moved into the area, and Broadway, the Great White Way,

*Clockwise from far left: Detail on the old Paramount Theater, a Times Square landmark; New Victory Theater, which specializes in family entertainment; bright lights, big city; New Year's Eve revelers; visitors flock to Times Square for shopping, family attractions and the full-on neon*

became synonymous with bigtime showbiz with its popular theatrical—especially musical—division. By 1914 there were some 43 theaters in the immediate vicinity of the square; after multiple closures, refurbishments and reopenings, there are 40 of them today.

**Best of Times, worst of Times** By the 1970s Times Square was decaying, many of the legitimate theaters having fallen on hard times and become porn theaters. But a massive clean-up effort in the 1990s brought about the area's rebirth. Today it's a tourist hotspot, with a raft of family attractions, megastores and restaurants beneath the glittering state-of-the-art illuminations. A large section of Times Square is now car-free, though the human traffic jams are bigger than ever.

## THE BASICS

timessquarenyc.org

🔠 D11

🚇 1, 2, 3, 7, N, Q, R, S Times Square–42nd Street

🚍 M5, M7, M20, M42, M104

❓ An audio-enhanced walking tour leaves several times daily from The Actors' Chapel (239 West 49th Street).

**TKTS Booth:** tdf.org/nyc/81/TKTS-Live provides real-time updates of what is on offer before you commit to standing in line

### HIGHLIGHTS

● Trinity Church
● Federal Hall
● New York Stock Exchange
● The House of Morgan

### TIP

● Weekend mornings are quietest in this part of town. To experience the hustle and bustle of Wall Street traders, come Mon–Fri around lunch.

Depending on your point of view, Wall Street is the boon or bane of the world's economic fortunes. But either way, the historic buildings and urban buzz of this financial powerhouse are fascinating to see and experience.

**The Buttonwood Agreement** Wall Street, named for the Dutch colonial wall that once marked the city's northern boundary, is the epicenter of the financial district. It has been so since the late 18th century, when businessmen gathered here under a buttonwood tree to trade bonds, issued to finance debts incurred in the Revolutionary War. In 1792, 24 traders signed the Buttonwood Agreement, which created the New York Stock Exchange. Today the NYSE is the largest stock exchange in the

*Clockwise from far left: The New York Stock Exchange; the soaring towers of Wall Street; Federal Hall, fronted by a bronze statue of George Washington and modeled on the Greek Parthenon; the beautifully decorated domed ceiling in the entrance of Federal Hall*

world. The 1903 building, with its grand trading floor and facade of Corinthian columns, stands at the corner with Broad Street.

**A million-dollar stroll** At the west end of Wall Street stands Trinity Church (1846), the third on this site. The original, built in 1699, was the city's first church. Alexander Hamilton and other famous New Yorkers are buried in the church-yard. At the corner of Wall and Broad streets sits the House of Morgan, once the most powerful financial institution in America (now housing apartments). George Washington was sworn in as America's first president at Federal Hall, now a national memorial and museum. Forty Wall Street is owned by Donald Trump. At No. 48, the Museum of American Finance has displays on financial history.

## THE BASICS

downtownny.com
nps.gov/feha
moaf.org
trinitywallstreet.org

✚ E22

✉ NYSE, 18 Broad Street; Federal Hall, 26 Wall Street; Museum of American Finance, 48 Wall Street; Trinity Church, Broadway at Wall Street

☎ Federal Hall 212/825-6990; Museum of American Finance 212/908-4110; Trinity Church 212/602-0800

🕐 Federal Hall Mon–Fri 9–5; Museum of American Finance Tue–Sat 10–4; Trinity Church Mon–Fri 7–6, Sat 8–4, Sun 7–4

🍴 Restaurants, pubs

🚇 2, 3, 4, 5 Wall Street; J, Z Broad Street 🚌 M5

♿ Federal Hall free; Museum of American Finance moderate; Trinity Church free

❓ Tours: Download Trinity Church's guided tour app from its website.

### HIGHLIGHTS

- Whitney Biennial
- *Brooklyn Bridge*, Joseph Stella (1939)
- Hoppers
- O'Keeffes
- *Dempsey and Firpo*, George Bellows (1924)
- Louise Nevelsons

### TIP

- Make certain you enjoy the museum's outdoor spaces, with great views of the Hudson, the High Line and Midtown.

Gertrude Vanderbilt Whitney's world-class collection, a showcase of her work and that of her friends, was first shown in a modest Greenwich Village studio space in 1918. Today, the collection is housed in the stunning and innovative Renzo Piano-designed headquarters along the High Line.

**No room at the Met** Sculptor and patron of her contemporaries' work, Gertrude Vanderbilt Whitney offered her collection of 700 modern artworks to the Met in 1929, but the great institution turned up its nose. Whitney instead formalized her own museum space, first in the Village, and then from 1966 to 2014 in Marcel Breuer's cantilevered headquarters on the Upper East Side. Having outgrown that space (now, ironically, an offshoot of the Met), the museum

*Left:* Dempsey and Firpo *by George Bellows (1924), a highlight of the Whitney's collection; right: The museum's new home is a 21st-century architectural gem*

moved in 2015 to Renzo Piano's dramatic new building in the Meatpacking District. The Whitney's collection reads like a roll call of American 20th-century greats: Edward Hopper, Thomas Hart Benton, Willem de Kooning, Georgia O'Keeffe, Claes Oldenburg, Jasper Johns, George Bellows and Jackson Pollock are perhaps the best known.

**Take your pick** Exhibitions, drawn from the museum's permanent collection, often emphasize a single artist's work. At other times they prove more eclectic. The Whitney Biennial (in the spring of even-numbered years) presents the curator's vision—sometimes controversial—of the leading trends in American art during the past two years and often features the work of young or lesser-known artists.

## THE BASICS

whitney.org

🔲 B16

✉ 99 Gansevoort Street/ Washington Street

☎ 212/570-3600

🕐 Sun–Mon, Wed–Thu 10.30–6, Fri–Sat 10.30–10

🍴 Restaurant, café

🚇 A, C, E 14th Street; L 8th Avenue

🚌 M14

♿ Excellent

✋ Expensive (under 18s free); donation Fri 7–10pm

❓ Free daily tours

### HIGHLIGHTS

- Memorial waterfalls
- One World Observatory
- 9/11 Museum
- One World Trade Center
- Transportation Hub
(the most expensive train station ever)

### TIP

- While admission to the museum and to the observatory are expensive, it is free at all times to visit the memorial.

The twin towers of the World Trade Center, once the tallest buildings in the world, were a New York icon until they were destroyed by terrorists who crashed two hijacked planes into them on September 11, 2001. From the ashes, a moving memorial has risen that pays tribute to those who lost their lives in the tragedy.

**The National September 11 Memorial and Museum** An international contest was held to select a fitting memorial for the site. Architects Michael Arad and Peter Walker's design, entitled "Reflecting Absence," was chosen. It comprises two square waterfalls, situated over the footprint of the towers. The waterfalls cascade 30ft (9m) into pools that disappear into a center void. The pools are surrounded by bronze

Clockwise from far left: Waterfalls at the National September 11 Memorial; One World Observatory; red and white roses on one of the inscribed bronze panels around the reflecting pools; the National September 11 Memorial from above

## THE BASICS

911memorial.org
oneworldobservatory.com
🔲 D21
✉ Church–West streets, Vesey–Liberty streets
☎ Memorial and museum: 212/266-5211; observatory: 844/696-1776
🕐 Memorial: daily 7.30am–9pm; museum: Sun–Thu 9–8 (last entry at 6), Fri–Sat 9–9 (last entry at 7); observatory: daily 9–8; longer in summer
🚇 E World Trade Center, A, C, J, Z, 2, 3, 4, 5 Fulton Street
🚌 M5, M20, M22
♿ Good
📱 Memorial free; museum and observatory expensive

panels inscribed with the names of almost 3,000 known victims of both this and a bomb attack on the towers in 1993. A memorial park with more than 300 oak trees provides a peaceful space for contemplation. The museum provides a history of the site and displays relics from the original World Trade Center, including the last column of steel to be removed from the rubble.

**One World Observatory** Atop One World Trade Center (presently America's tallest building) is One World Observatory, with 360-degree views of Manhattan, Brooklyn, New York Harbor, and beyond. "Sky Pods" (elevators) with stunning animations of Manhattan's 400-year development whisk visitors up to the 100th-story view in 60 seconds.

# More to See

This section contains other great places to visit if you have more time. Some are in the heart of the city while others are a short journey away, found under Farther Afield. This chapter also has fantastic excursions that you should set aside a whole day to visit.

**In the Heart of the City** 66

American Folk Art Museum 66

Battery Park 66

Brooklyn Bridge 66

Chelsea Gallery District 66

Chrysler Building 67

City Hall 67

Eldridge Street Synagogue 67

Flatiron Building 68

Grace Church 68

Italian American Museum 68

Jewish Museum 68

Lower East Side
Tenement Museum 68

Met Breuer 69

Morgan Library
& Museum 69

El Museo del Barrio 69

Museum of Arts
and Design 70

Museum of Chinese
in America 70

Museum of the City
of New York 70

Neue Galerie 70

New Museum of
Contemporary Art 71

New-York Historical Society 71

Rubin Museum of Art 71

St. Patrick's Cathedral 71

St. Patrick's Old Cathedral 72

St. Paul's Chapel 72

South Street Seaport 72

Trump Tower 73

Union Square 73

United Nations
Headquarters 73

U.S. Custom House 73

Washington Square 73

**Farther Afield** 74

Bronx Zoo 74

The Cloisters 74

Coney Island 74

Flushing Meadows–
Corona Park 75

Harlem 75

Staten Island 75

Yankee Stadium 75

# In the Heart of the City

### AMERICAN FOLK ART MUSEUM

folkartmuseum.org

The outstanding collection of quilts is a highlight in this museum spanning the rich variety of folk art, from paintings and pottery to textiles and woodcarving; exhibits date from the 18th century to the present day. The museum's shop stocks a superb range of handcrafted items.

🞚 C8 ✉ 2 Lincoln Square (Columbus Avenue between 65th and 66th streets) ☎ 212/595-9533 🕐 Tue–Thu, Sat 11.30–7, Fri 12–7.30, Sun 12–6 🚇 1 66th Street–Lincoln Center 🎟 Free

### BATTERY PARK

thebattery.org

At the southernmost tip of Manhattan, with splendid views of New York Harbor, Battery Park was named for the cannon sited here to defend the fledgling city against British attack. Ferries to the Statue of Liberty and Ellis Island leave from Castle Clinton National Monument, a former fort. Among the monuments in the park, look for *The Sphere*, which once stood at the World Trade Center plaza and serves as a memorial to 9/11. An aquatic carousel stands at the park's southern end.

🞚 E23 ✉ Tip of Manhattan 🚇 1 South Ferry; 4, 5 Bowling Green

### BROOKLYN BRIDGE

Completed in 1883, the Brooklyn Bridge was the first to link Manhattan and Brooklyn. With its twin Gothic towers and graceful ballet of cables, it is one of New York's finest landmarks. Stroll across the pedestrian walkway for views of the Manhattan skyline.

🞚 G21 🚇 4, 5, 6 Brooklyn Bridge–City Hall; A, C High Street/Brooklyn Bridge

### CHELSEA GALLERY DISTRICT

When real estate prices in SoHo began to skyrocket in the 1990s, the downtown galleries moved to Chelsea. Today, there are over 100 galleries in the neighborhood, primarily located between 10th and 11th avenues. Most galleries are closed on Mondays, but almost everything is open both days of

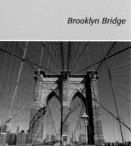

*The American Folk Art Museum*

*Brooklyn Bridge*

the weekend. Gallery hopping, you can take in everything from established artists to Modernist masters to stars of the up-and-coming generation.
➕ B14 ✉ From 30th Street south to 14th Street, and 9th Avenue west to the Hudson River 🚇 1, 14th, 18th, 23rd, 28th streets–7th Avenue; C, E 14th, 23rd streets–8th Avenue

## CHRYSLER BUILDING

The gleaming art deco spire of the Chrysler Building is an iconic symbol of New York. When completed in 1931, it held the title of "world's tallest building" until it was surpassed by the Empire State Building the same year. Every detail of the 77-story building evokes a 1929 Chrysler Plymouth. The winged steel gargoyles are modeled on its radiator caps; the building's stepped setbacks carry stylized hubcaps and the spire resembles a radiator grille. You can visit the lobby to see the art deco detailing in the red marble, granite and chrome interior, surmounted by the 97ft by 100ft (30m by

*The Chrysler Building*

31m) mural depicting industrial scenes and celebrating "transportation." Don't miss the art deco marquetry on the elevator doors.
➕ F11 ✉ 405 Lexington Avenue/42nd Street 🕐 Mon–Fri office hours 🚇 4, 5, 6, 7, S Grand Central–42nd Street 🚌 M101, M102, M103, M42 🚆 Metro North, Grand Central 🚹 Good 🎟 Free

## CITY HALL

nyc.gov/html/artcom
Built between 1803 and 1812 in Federal and French Renaissance styles, this is one of the nation's oldest city halls. The building and the rotunda, with its Corinthian columns and coffered dome, are designated landmarks. See the Governor's Room furniture and portrait collection on a guided tour.
➕ E21 ✉ Broadway/Murray Street ☎ 311 or 212/639-9675 🕐 Wed (admission on a first come, first served basis) and Thu (advance reservations required) 🚇 2, 3 Park Place; 4, 5, 6 Brooklyn Bridge–City Hall; R City Hall 🎟 Free

## ELDRIDGE STREET SYNAGOGUE

eldridgestreet.org
Built in 1887, this synagogue is a symbol of the aspirations of Eastern European immigrants on the Lower East Side. Its 50ft (15m) vaulted ceiling, Moorish and Romanesque details and stained-glass windows make it one of the city's architectural gems. Exhibits and guided tours point out design features and tell the story of this diverse neighborhood.
➕ G19 ✉ 12 Eldridge Street ☎ 212/219-0302 🕐 Sun–Thu 10–5, Fri 10–3 🚇 F East Broadway; B, D Grand Street 🎟 Moderate

## FLATIRON BUILDING

This 1902 skyscraper designed by Daniel Burnham was named for its amazing and memorable shape. It is an isosceles triangle with a sharp angle pointing uptown.

E14 ✉ 175 5th Avenue/E 22nd–23rd streets N, R 23rd Street

## GRACE CHURCH

gracechurchnyc.org

This early James Renwick-designed Gothic Revival church dating from the mid-19th century has superb stained glass windows and a mosaic floor.

E–F16 ✉ 802 Broadway ☎ 212/254-2000 Mon–Sat 12–5, Sun services N, R 8th Street–NYU; 6 Astor Place Free guided tours Sun 1pm

## ITALIAN AMERICAN MUSEUM

italianamericanmuseum.org

In the heart of Little Italy, this small museum explores the history and heritage of America's Italian immigrants. Exhibits range from New York policeman Frank Serpico's guns to a collection of marionettes from the 1920s and 1930s.

F19 ✉ 155 Mulberry Street/Grand Street ☎ 212/965-9000 Mon–Fri 12–6 N, R Prince Street; F, V Broadway–Lafayette Donation

## JEWISH MUSEUM

thejewishmuseum.org

The largest Jewish museum in the Western hemisphere chronicles Jewish experiences worldwide. Artifacts in the permanent collection cover 4,000 years of Jewish history, while special exhibitions focus on Jewish culture and more.

E4 ✉ 1109 5th Avenue/92nd Street ☎ 212/423-3200 Sat–Tue 11–5.45, Thu 11–8, Fri (Mar–Oct) 11–5.45, closing earlier Nov–Feb Café 4, 5, 6 86th Street Expensive; free Sat

## LOWER EAST SIDE TENEMENT MUSEUM

tenement.org

This reconstruction of life in an 1863 tenement block is a must for history buffs. Tours focus on the homes and workshops of Jewish, Italian and Irish immigrants, and there are also walking tours of the neighborhood.

*The Italian American Museum documents the rich history of Little Italy*

⊞ G18  ✉ 103 Orchard Street
☎ 212/982-8420  ⏱ Tours daily 10–5,
visitor center Fri–Wed 10–6.30, Thu 10–8.30
Ⓜ F, J, M, Z Delancey Street–Essex Street;
B, D Grand Street  💲 Expensive

## MET BREUER

metmuseum.org

When the Whitney Museum decamped for Chelsea from its Marcel Breuer-designed headquarters uptown, the Metropolitan Museum scooped up the property to showcase modern and contemporary artwork. Using the Met's own collection as a starting point, the new satellite campus (free with paid admission to the nearby Fifth Avenue building) brings together artwork from around the world, and places newer pieces in the context of work stretching back to the Renaissance. Download *Soundwalk 9:09* by John Luther Adams to listen to as you walk between the two buildings.

⊞ E7  ✉ 945 Madison Avenue/E 75th Street  ☎ 212/535-7710  ⏱ Tue–Wed, Sat–Sun 10–5.30, Thu–Fri 10–9  Ⓜ 6 77th Street  💲 Expensive

## MORGAN LIBRARY & MUSEUM

themorgan.org

This collection of literary works, rare musical manuscripts and artworks was amassed by financier J.P. Morgan. Highlights here include the ninth-century Lindau Gospels, a vellum copy of the Gutenberg Bible, music scores by Beethoven, Mozart and Puccini, etchings by Raphael and Michelangelo and manuscripts by Charles Dickens and Mark Twain.

⊞ E12  ✉ 225 Madison Avenue/E 36th Street  ☎ 212/685-0008  ⏱ Tue–Thu 10.30–5, Fri 10.30–9, Sat 10–6, Sun 11–6  Ⓜ 6 33rd Street; 4, 5, 6 7 Grand Central  💲 Expensive

## EL MUSEO DEL BARRIO

elmuseo.org

This museum dedicated to Latin American and Caribbean art contains over 8,000 items from pre-Columbian artifacts to modern paintings and photographs. There is also a program of events.

⊞ E2  ✉ 1230 5th Avenue/104th Street  ☎ 212/831-7272  ⏱ Tue–Sat 11–6  Ⓜ 6 103rd Street  💲 Moderate

*New York's Jewish Museum chronicles the history of Jews worldwide*

## MUSEUM OF ARTS AND DESIGN

madmuseum.org

Affectionaly known as MAD, the museum showcases crafts, art and design through an impressive permanent collection, special exhibitions and public programs, while the monthly Studio Sundays allow families to get involved in creative activities.

➕ C9 ✉ 2 Columbus Circle ☎ 212/299-2777 🕐 Sat–Sun, Tue–Wed 10–6, Thu–Fri 10–9 🍽 Restaurant 🚇 1, A, C, B, D 59th Street–Columbus Circle ♿ Expensive (by donation Thu 6–9pm)

## MUSEUM OF CHINESE IN AMERICA

mocanyc.org

The permanent collection tells the story of Chinese immigration across the USA. Temporary exhibits examine aspects of the contemporary Chinese-American experience.

➕ F19 ✉ 215 Centre Street/Grand Street ☎ 212/619-4785 🕐 Tue–Wed, Fri–Sun 11–6, Thu 11–9 🚇 6, N, Q, R, J, Z Canal Street ♿ Moderate

## MUSEUM OF THE CITY OF NEW YORK

mcny.org

Rotating exhibitions here illustrate the ever-changing life of the city since 1624. It has an outstanding collection of photographs, as well as toys, furniture and decorative arts. Special walking tours are available also.

➕ E2 ✉ 1220 5th Avenue/103rd Street ☎ 212/534-1672 🕐 Daily 10–6 🚇 6 103rd Street ♿ Expensive

## NEUE GALERIE

neuegalerie.org

Dedicated to early 20th-century German and Austrian art and design, the highlight is Gustav Klimt's portrait *Adele Bloch-Bauer I* (1907). European decorative arts and the Bauhaus are also well represented in the permanent collection, with contributions from the likes of Marcel Breuer and Walter Gropius.

➕ E5 ✉ 1048 5th Avenue/86th Street ☎ 212/628-6200 🕐 Thu–Mon 11–6 🍽 Café 🚇 4, 5, 6 86th Street ♿ Expensive

Neue Galerie

## NEW MUSEUM OF CONTEMPORARY ART

newmuseum.org

The dynamic building resembling giant white boxes stacked askew is a fitting home for this cutting-edge museum of contemporary art. The seventh-floor balcony affords panoramic views out over Lower Manhattan.

🏠 F18 ✉ 235 Bowery/Prince Street ☎ 212/219-1222 🕐 Wed–Sun 11–6, Thu 11–9 🍴 Café 🚇 N, R Prince Street 💷 Expensive

## NEW-YORK HISTORICAL SOCIETY

nyhistory.org

With 1.6 million objects dating from the Dutch Colonial era to the tragic events of 9/11, the society's permanent collection and temporary exhibitions reveal key chapters in New York's past. Admission includes the film *New York Story*, an immersive, 18-minute narrative of the city's growth from Dutch trading port to world economic powerhouse. Many key objects are on view just inside the main entrance, including fragments from America's first capitol building and the shackles of a child who was held in slavery.

🏠 C6 ✉ Central Park West/77th Street ☎ 212/873-3400 🕐 Tue–Thu and Sat 10–6, Fri 10–8, Sun 11–5 🚇 B/C 81st Street 💷 Expensive

## RUBIN MUSEUM OF ART

rubinmuseum.org

The superb collection of art from Tibet and the Himalayan region is the largest in the West. Religious art and cultural artifacts include scroll paintings, sculptures, ritual objects, textiles, masks and prints.

🏠 D15 ✉ 150 W 17th Street/7th Avenue ☎ 212/620-5000 🕐 Mon, Thu 11–5, Wed 11–9, Fri 11–10, Sat–Sun 11–6 🍴 Café 🚇 1 18th Street–7th Avenue 💷 Expensive, free Fri 6–10

## ST. PATRICK'S CATHEDRAL

saintpatrickscathedral.org

With its ornate spires soaring 330ft (100m) above Fifth Avenue, James Renwick's Gothic Revival cathedral, built in 1858–79, seats 2,200 people. The St. Michael and

*The New-York Historical Society*

*The dynamic New Museum of Contemporary Art*

St. Louis altar was designed by Tiffany & Co., while the rose window is one of stained-glass artist Charles Connick's finest creations.

⊞ E10 ✉ 5th Avenue between E 50th and E 51st streets ☎ 212/753-2261 ⊙ Daily 6.30am–8.45pm; services at various times 🚇 6 51st Street; E, M 5th Avenue–53rd Street ✋ Free

## ST. PATRICK'S OLD CATHEDRAL

oldcathedral.org

New York's first Roman Catholic cathedral opened in 1815, when the area was settled by Irish immigrants. The building, restored in 1868, has a stunning hand-carved altarpiece filled with statuary.

⊞ F18 ✉ Mott Street between Prince and Houston streets ☎ 212/226-8075 (call for times) ⊙ Daily, hours may vary 🚇 N, R, Prince Street ✋ Free

## ST. PAUL'S CHAPEL

trinitywallstreet.org

Opened in 1766, this is the only remaining Colonial-era church to be found in Manhattan. George Washington worshiped here after his inauguration. St. Paul's escaped destruction on 9/11 and became a round-the-clock refuge for rescue workers. In the churchyard is the Bell of Hope, a gift from the City of London on the first anniversary of the tragedy.

⊞ F21 ✉ 209 Broadway at Fulton Street ☎ 212/602-0800 ⊙ Mon–Sat 10–6, churchyard 10–4, Sun 7–6, churchyard 7–3.30 🚇 2, 3, 4, 5, A, C, J, Z Fulton Street ✋ Free

## SOUTH STREET SEAPORT

southstreetseaport.com

In the midst of a post-Hurricane Sandy transformation, South Street Seaport is smaller than it once was, but still worth exploring. The collection of the South Street Seaport Museum includes a number of historic ships. There are dining and shopping options here and an outpost of the Times Square TKTS ticket booth (▷ 56) with a much smaller line than its uptown sibling.

⊞ G21 ✉ Fulton Street at Water Street ☎ Museum 212/748-8600 🚇 2, 3, 4, 5, A, C, J, Z Fulton Street

*The flags of member nations flying high at the United Nations Headquarters*

## TRUMP TOWER

trump.com

Ride the escalators to admire the 1980s glitz and glamor in all its glory. The six-story atrium is filled with shops, greenery and waterfalls, while the top floors include the Donald Trump's own penthouse and the boardroom used in the US version of the TV show *The Apprentice*.

✛ E9 ⊠ 725 5th Avenue/56th Street ☎ 212/832-2000 ⏰ Daily 8am–10pm ⍞ Several ⓢ N, Q, R 5th Avenue–59th Street; E, M, 5th Avenue–53rd Street

## UNION SQUARE

Named for the union of Broadway and Fourth Avenue, this is where downtown and uptown meet. It is ringed with shops and restaurants and four days a week has the city's best greenmarket, selling home-grown produce (▷ 125).

✛ E15 ⊠ E 14th–17th streets, Park Avenue South, Broadway ⏰ Greenmarket Mon, Wed, Fri, Sat 8–6 ⍞ Numerous ⓢ 4, 5, 6, L, N, Q, R 14th Street–Union Square ⊟ M3 ♿ Good

## UNITED NATIONS HEADQUARTERS

visit.un.org

Take a guided tour to see the General Assembly Hall and collection of art and artifacts donated from around the world. A limited number of same-day tickets are available on site, but it's much better to buy them online in advance. Arrive at least 30 minutes early for security screening.

✛ G11 ⊠ 1st Avenue/45th–46th streets ☎ 212/963-8687 ⏰ Mon–Fri 9–4.30 (a guided tour ticket is required) ⍞ Café, restaurant ⓢ 4, 5, 6, 7 to Grand Central 🎟 Expensive

## US CUSTOM HOUSE

nmai.si.edu/visit/newyork/

Also known as the Alexander Hamilton US Custom House, this 1907 Beaux Arts beauty, designed by Cass Gilbert, now houses the Smithsonian's National Museum of the American Indian, highlighting native cultures of North, Central and South America.

✛ E23 ⊠ 1 Bowling Green ☎ 212/514-3700 ⏰ Museum daily 10–5 ⓢ 4, 5 Bowling Green; 1 South Ferry 🎟 Free

## WASHINGTON SQUARE

nycgovparks.org/parks/washington-square-park

The square is a prime people-watching spot in Greenwich Village. At the north end, Washington Memorial Arch, designed by Stanford White, marks the start of Fifth Avenue. Notice "The Row" of Greek Revival homes (Nos. 1–13) where the elite of 19th-century New York lived. If you want to get a real feel, read Henry James's *Washington Square*.

✛ E17 ⓢ N, R 8th Street–NYU; A, B, C, D, E, F, M 4th Street–Washington Square

*The US Custom House*

# Farther Afield

## BRONX ZOO

bronxzoo.com

The biggest city zoo in the US has over 4,000 animals and is a leader in wildlife conservation. Don't miss the Congo Gorilla Forest, or the Wild Asia Complex with its mono-rail riding high above tigers, rhinos and elephants.

➕ See map ▷ 111  ✉ Fordham Road (Bronx River Parkway Northeast)
☎ 718/367-1010  🕐 Apr–Oct daily 10–5; Nov–Mar 10–4.30  🍴 Restaurant
🚇 2 Pelham Parkway  💲 Expensive (Wed discounts)

## THE CLOISTERS

metmuseum.org/visit/visit-the-cloisters/

A 12th-century Spanish apse attached to a Romanesque cloister and a Gothic chapel—what's all this doing in Upper Manhattan? This is the Met's medieval branch. The bulk of the art and architecture, which is arranged chronologically, was amassed by sculptor George Gray Barnard in the early 20th century. Much was rescued from ruin. The effigy of the Crusader Jean d'Alluye, for instance, was doing duty as a bridge, while the priceless Unicorn tapestries were acting as frost blankets.

➕ See map ▷ 111  ✉ Fort Tryon Park, North Manhattan  ☎ 212/923-3700
🕐 Mar–Oct daily 10–5.15; Nov–Feb 10–4.45  🚇 A 190th Street  💲 Expensive (Met Museum admission includes entry to the Cloisters)

## CONEY ISLAND

coneyisland.com

At the end of the 19th century, Coney Island on a peak day played host to a million people. Since then, attractions have come and gone but the big dipper ride, the Cyclone, is still here and Nathan's Famous hot dogs are still sold from the original site. A newer attraction is MCU Park, home of the Brooklyn Cyclones baseball team, which also hosts concerts. Also on Coney Island is the New York Aquarium. A slew of new amusement parks are revitalizing the area and restoring its charm.

➕ See map ▷ 110  ✉ Surf Avenue, Boardwalk; Aquarium: W 8th Street, Surf

*Bronx Zoo, the largest city zoo in the US*

*One of the set of late 15th-century Flemish Unicorn tapestries on display at the Cloisters*

Avenue 🐟 Aquarium 718/265-3474
🕐 Jun–early Sep daily 10–6, Sep–May
10–4.30 🍴 Cafés 🚇 D, F, N, Q Coney
Island–Stillwell Avenue 💲 Aquarium
moderate, rides expensive

## FLUSHING MEADOWS–CORONA PARK

The attractions here are the New
York Hall of Science and Queens
Museum of Art. The former is a
hands-on science and technology
museum with a great Science
Playground for kids (4701 111th
Street, tel 718/699-0005, nysci.
org). The Queens Museum of Art
(New York Building, tel 718/592-
9700, queensmuseum.org) holds
a scale panorama of New York.
Outside stands the Unisphere—
the world's largest globe. In late
summer, the US Open tennis
tournament is played in Arthur
Ashe Stadium.
➕ See map ▷ 111

## HARLEM

The capital of black culture in
America during the Harlem
Renaissance in the 1920s, the
neighborhood is going through
a 21st-century rebirth, with
skyrocketing real estate prices.
Music lovers should check out
the Apollo Theater (253 W 125th
Street, tel 212/531-5300) for
big-name acts or the famous
amateur showcase. Nearby, the
Studio Museum in Harlem (144 W
125th Street, tel 212/864-4500)
displays contemporary art and
retrospectives. Historic exhibits are
mounted at the Schomburg Center
for Research in Black Culture
(515 Malcolm X Boulevard, tel
917/275-6975).
➕ See map ▷ 110

## STATEN ISLAND

There are several historic sights
here. Alice Austen House (2 Hylan
Boulevard, tel 718/816-4506,
aliceausten.org) is a museum of
photographs by Alice Austen in
her colonial home. Historic
Richmond Town (441 Clarke
Avenue, tel 718/351-1611,
historicrichmondtown.org)
recreates daily life in a 19th-
century village.
➕ See map ▷ 110

## YANKEE STADIUM

yankees.mlb.com
The Yankees dominated the
early era of baseball. In 1920,
Babe Ruth joined the team and
quickly became a hero. The team
clinched the World Series title in
1996, 1998, 1999, 2000 and
2009, the year they moved into
their new Yankee Stadium.
➕ See map ▷ 111 ✉ E 161st
Street, Bronx ☎ 718/293-4300
🕐 Season runs Apr–Oct. Check
schedule for games 🍴 Concession
stands 🚇 4, B, D 161st Street/Yankee
Stadium 💲 Expensive

*The Yankee Stadium in the Bronx,
home of the New York Yankees*

# City Tours

This section contains self-guided tours that will help you explore the sights in each of the city's regions. Each tour is designed to take a day, with a map pinpointing the recommended places along the way. There is a quick reference guide at the end of each tour, listing everything you need in that region, so you know exactly what's close by.

Lower Manhattan      **78**

Downtown and Chelsea      **84**

Midtown      **90**

Upper East Side and Central Park      **96**

Upper West Side      **102**

Farther Afield      **108**

**CITY TOURS**

# Lower Manhattan

The cradle of New York, Lower Manhattan is steeped in history—new immigrants landed here from the 17th century until the early 20th century. This area is also home to the Financial District, historic Seaport and fashionable SoHo.

**Morning**
Start the day at the tip of Manhattan in **Battery Park** (▷ 66), with its splendid views of New York Harbor. Ferries for the **Statue of Liberty** (▷ 54–55) and **Ellis Island** (▷ 26–27) leave from Castle Clinton, but save these for a separate day. Cross State Street to admire the beautiful Beaux Arts facade of the **US Custom House** (▷ 73), housing the National Museum of the American Indian. Then proceed along Bowling Green, the small square opposite, past the Charging Bull statue (right), a symbol of Wall Street.

**Mid-morning**
Walk up Broadway and note the plaques for over a century of ticker tape parades. Continue north to visit the **World Trade Center** (▷ 62–63). Farther south, **Trinity Church** (left; ▷ 59) marks the west end of **Wall Street** (▷ 58–59); stroll around the old churchyard, then head down Wall Street to **Federal Hall**, the **New York Stock Exchange** and other sites.

**Lunch**
Rub shoulders with Financial District workers and have a pub lunch at **The Bailey Pub & Brasserie** (▷ 142), one block north of Wall Street. The *steak frites* is delicious, or try a hearty *plat du jour* such as shepherd's pie.

**CITY TOURS**

### Afternoon
Walk north on Front Street to **South Street Seaport** (▷ 72). From the waterfront along the East River there are good views of **Brooklyn Bridge** (▷ 66). Follow Dover Street west to **City Hall** (▷ 67), then take Centre Street north into **Chinatown** (▷ 20–21). Explore its bustling markets, its quiet temples and herbalist shops. Explore the culture of this area in depth with a stop at the **Museum of Chinese in America** (▷ 70), which details the experiences of these immigrants.

### Mid-afternoon
Chinatown spills north into **Little Italy**. Walk north on Mulberry Street, past the **Italian American Museum** (▷ 68), and when you reach **St. Patrick's Old Cathedral** (▷ 72), turn left on Prince Street, which will bring you into **SoHo** (▷ 52–53). Grab a coffee at **Dean & DeLuca** (▷ 52) to keep you going as you browse the art galleries, ogle the cast-iron buildings and indulge in some shopping. Most stores here stay open into early evening.

### Evening
There are plenty of ultra-chic bars in SoHo for a cocktail or a nightcap. For some old SoHo atmosphere, try **Fanelli's** (94 Prince Street, between Mercer and Greene streets, tel 212/226-9412).

### Dinner
After drinks, make your way east to **Delicatessen** (▷ 144), where they serve updated versions of classic comfort food. There's great SoHo people-watching from its outdoor tables. If you want something even more old-school, make **Lombardi's** (32 Spring Street at Mott Street, tel 212/941-7994) your destination. It was the first sit-down pizzeria in America.

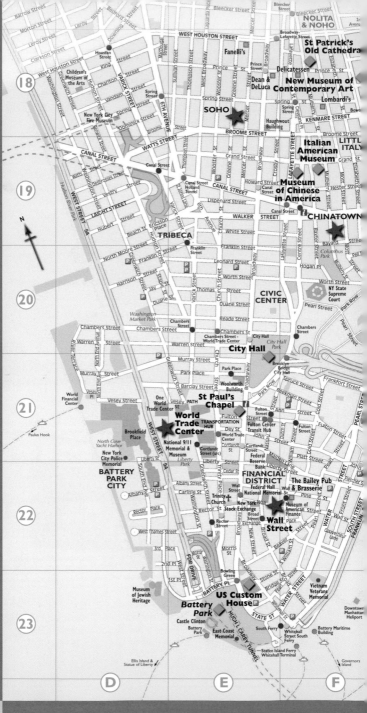

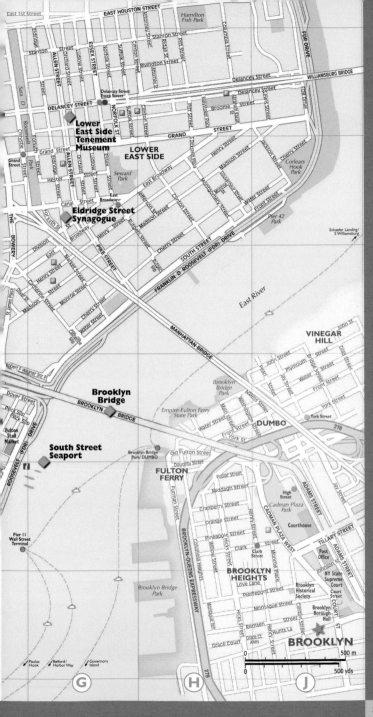

# **Lower Manhattan** Quick Reference Guide

**TOP 25** SIGHTS AND EXPERIENCES

### Chinatown (▷ 20)
Explore this bustling neighborhood of streetside produce stalls, herbalist shops, Buddhist temples, dim sum parlors and tempting restaurants.

### Ellis Island (▷ 26)
Follow in the footsteps of millions of immigrants, most of whom traveled in cramped steerage class, who passed through this gateway to New York and the New World.

### SoHo (▷ 52)
SoHo features leading art galleries, trendy boutiques, top fashion chains, cool bars and chic restaurants in 19th-century cast-iron buildings.

### Statue of Liberty (▷ 54)
A visit to this iconic landmark is a must on any visit to New York. The ferry ride to the island is impressive, and the view from the statue's crown is breathtaking.

### Wall Street (▷ 58)
During Dutch colonial times, Wall Street marked the northern boundary of New York. Now home to bankers and brokers, it's the powerhouse of the US economy.

### World Trade Center (▷ 62)
The National September 11 Memorial, on the site of the Twin Towers, is both impressive and poignant. It's a quiet place for peace and contemplation.

## MORE TO SEE     64

Battery Park
Brooklyn Bridge
City Hall
Eldridge Street Synagogue
Italian American Museum
Lower East Side Tenement Museum
Museum of Chinese in America
New Museum of Contemporary Art
St. Patrick's Old Cathedral
St. Paul's Chapel
South Street Seaport
US Custom House

## SHOP     114

**Books**
The Mysterious Bookshop
**Clothes**
Abercrombie & Fitch
Resurrection
**Discount**
Century 21

**Food and Wine**
The Pickle Guys
**Homewares**
New Kam Man
**Shoes**
Alife Rivington Club

## ENTERTAINMENT     126

**Bars**
The Dead Rabbit Grocery and Grog
Parkside Lounge
The Porterhouse
   at Fraunces Tavern
Wassail
**Cinema**
Film Forum

**Clubs**
Arlene's Grocery
Beach at Governors Island
S.O.B.'s
**Comedy**
Comedy Cellar
**Live Music**
City Winery

## EAT     138

**Asian**
Mission Chinese
Nobu
Vegetarian Dim Sum
**Casual**
The Bailey Pub & Brasserie
Bubby's

Delicatessen
Schillers
**Classic NY**
Katz's Deli
Odeon

# Downtown and Chelsea

The area from Houston Street north to 30th Street encompasses NoHo and the East Village, the tree-lined streets of Greenwich Village, the Meatpacking District with its trendy stores and clubs, and Chelsea, home of the High Line and the Whitney Museum of American Art.

### Morning
Start the day with breakfast at one of the bakeries in **Chelsea Market** (right; ▷ 121). You can either eat there or take it with you up to the **High Line** (▷ 40). Begin your explorations on this converted railbed by heading north, but eventually wend your way to the Gansevoort Street end of the park and the **Whitney Museum of American Art** (▷ 60).

### Late morning/lunch
Leave the High Line at its southern terminus and strike out for the heart of the Village along Bleecker Street. If you need a snack, you'll pass **Magnolia Bakery** (401 Bleecker Street), made (in)famous by the TV show *Sex and the City*. When Bleecker Street reaches MacDougal Street, head north. These blocks were the epicenter of the early '60s folk scene. You'll soon reach **Washington Square** (▷ 73) which is a great place for people-watching. But first, lunch! The bistro-style **North Square Restaurant** (▷ 147) in the **Washington Square Hotel** (▷ 159) is a good choice for Mediterranean dishes.

### Afternoon
After lunch, stroll through Washington Square to its southern side (West 4th Street) and begin walking east to the **East Village** (▷ 24–25). **The Merchant's House Museum** is a fascinating look back at an earlier era, complete with furnishings that were moved into the house in the 1830s. Then make your way up to **St. Mark's Place** (E 8th Street) with its funky mix of ethnic restaurants and shops.

### Late afternoon
From the East Village head back to Broadway and the **Strand Bookstore** (▷ 125) and **Grace Church** (▷ 68) which has free audio tours via mobile phone. Just a few blocks north of the church is **Union Square** (left, ▷ 73). Visit on a Monday, Wednesday, Friday or Saturday, and you'll be able to browse the food stands of **Union Square Greenmarket** (▷ 125).

### Evening
For a historic watering hole, head for the **White Horse Tavern** (▷ 137) on Hudson Street, where poet Dylan Thomas drank his last. Or head up to 23rd Street: At Fifth Avenue is **Eataly** (▷ 121), which has imported Italian goods and fine restaurants. It stands in the shadow of the Flatiron Building (▷ 68), New York's best early skyscraper.

### Dinner
If you're not dining at Eataly, head to the Meatpacking District (below right) for **Fatty Crab** (▷ 145), where high-end cocktails meet riffs on Malaysian street food.

### Late evening
After dinner, you are spoiled for choice. Stay in the Meatpacking District or head back to the West Village for cool jazz at the **Blue Note** (▷ 132) or the **Village Vanguard** (178 7th Avenue South at W 11th Street, tel 212/255-4037). The clubs on Bleecker and MacDougal Street feature live music, too, with **Le Poisson Rouge** (158 Bleecker, tel 212/505-3474) drawing a wide range of acts, from classical trios to world music to cult bands.

Midtown/W 39th St
West 39th Street
West 38th Street
LINCOLN TUNNEL 495
West 37th Street
GARMENT DISTRICT
Jacob Javits Convention Center
West 36th Street
West 35th Street
Pier 76
34th Street Penn Station
WEST 34TH STREET
34th Street Penn Station
Macy's
34th Street Herald Square
West 33rd Street
HUDSON YARDS
34th Street/Hudson Yards
Area under redevelopment
Madison Square Garden
PENN STATION
West 31st Street
West 30th Street
West 30th Street
WEST 30TH STREET
West 30th Street
West 29th Street
West 28th Street
West 28th Street
Chelsea Park
MANHATTAN
West 27th Street
West 26th Street
CHELSEA GALLERY DITRICT
West 25th Street
West 24th Street
CHELSEA
High Line
West 23rd Street
23rd Street
23rd Street
West 23rd St
23rd Street
West 22nd Street
Chelsea Hotel
West 21st Street
Chelsea Waterside Park
West 20th Street
West 19th Street
West 18th Street
18th Street
West 17th Street
Chelsea Piers
West 16th Street
Rubin Museum of Art
West 15th Street
Chelsea Market
MEATPACKING DISTRICT
WEST 14TH STREET
14th Street
14th Street
14th Street
8th Avenue
6th Avenue
West 13th Street
Fatty Crab
Little West 12th Street
Bloomfield St
WEST VILLAGE
Whitney Museum of American Art
Village Vanguard
Jane Street
Magnolia Bakery
Bethune Street
White Horse Tavern
Bank Street
Waverly
West 11th Street
Perry Street
Christopher Street Sheridan Square
West Washington Place
Charles Street
West 10th Street
GREENWICH VILLAGE
Hudson River
West 4th Street
Barrow Street
Morton Street
Leroy Street
Clarkson Street
West Houston Street
Houston Street
Children's Museum of the Arts
Charlton Street
Pier 40
New York City Fire Museum

11TH AVENUE
10th Avenue
9th Avenue
8th Avenue
7th Avenue
6th Avenue
Broadway
12TH AVENUE
9A
West 30th Street Heliport

N

12
13
14
15
16
17
18

B
C
D

# Downtown and Chelsea
## Quick Reference Guide

**CITY TOURS**

### East Village and NoHo (▷ 24)
The East Village, with its immigrant history and counterculture vibe, is well worth exploring. Nearby NoHo, once one of the most elegant residential neighborhoods in the city, still features beautiful homes and cobblestone streets.

### Greenwich Village (▷ 36)
Once an actual village, this area has gorgeous, tree-lined streets. It was the center of the folk revival of the 1960s, birthplace of the gay rights movement, and has been home to generations of artists and writers.

### High Line (▷ 40)
Local residents banded together to turn this abandoned elevated railbed into one of New York's premier parks. The park has attracted shops, restaurants, and high-end apartment construction, while still retaining its charm.

### Whitney Museum of American Art (▷ 60)
One of the finest collections of 20th-century American art, the Whitney has expanded its scope with a move from the Upper East Side to the Meatpacking District, while still showcasing the permanent collection that made it famous.

## MORE TO SEE 64

Chelsea Gallery District
Flatiron Building
Grace Church
Rubin Museum of Art

Union Square
Washington Square

## SHOP 114

**Accessories**
Village Tannery
**Beauty**
C.O. Bigelow
Kiehl's
**Books**
Barnes & Noble
Strand
**Clothes**
Cynthia Rowley
Hotoveli
Jeffrey New York
Kenneth Cole

Marc Jacobs
Scoop
**Food and Wine**
Chelsea Market
Eataly
Union Square Greenmarket
**Homewares**
ABC Carpet and Home
**Shoes**
DSW
**Toys**
Kidding Around

## ENTERTAINMENT 126

**Bars**
McSorley's Old Ale House
Pete's Tavern
White Horse Tavern
**Cabaret**
Duplex (▷ panel, 134)
Joe's Pub
**Clubs**
Café Wha?
**Comedy**
Gotham Comedy Club

**Jazz**
Blue Note
**Karaoke**
Sing Sing Karaoke
**Live Music**
Mercury Lounge
**Theater/Performance**
Cherry Lane Theatre

## EAT 138

**Asian**
Fatty Crab
Ssäm Bar
**Contemporary**
Eleven Madison Park
Gotham Bar and Grill
North Square
The Spotted Pig

**French/American**
Almond
**Italian**
Del Posto
**Polish/Ukrainian**
Veselka

CITY TOURS

89

# Midtown

Midtown is a must for visitors. It has leading museums, pulsating Times Square, Grand Central Terminal plus the magnet for shoppers—Fifth Avenue. It also has three of New York's most famous skyscrapers, two with observatories for stupendous views.

### Morning
Get an early start at **Rockefeller Center** (▷ 50–51). The subway concourse below 30 Rockefeller Plaza is full of restaurants; pick up a coffee and breakfast sandwich at **'wichcraft**, or have a more substantial breakfast at the **Rock Center Café**, which looks out on the famous ice rink. Be sure to see the many beautiful artworks around the complex, before or after enjoying the observation decks at **Top of the Rock** (right) for majestic city views.

### Mid-morning
Walk west along 50th Street to **Radio City Music Hall** (▷ 136), and turn right up Sixth Avenue. Turn right on 53rd Street to visit the **Museum of Modern Art** (▷ 46–47).

### Lunch
"Quick" and "inexpensive" are foreign words in this part of Midtown. Your best bet for a simple lunch that won't break the bank is to head to the **Halal Guys**, who operate their renowned food carts at the corner of 53rd Street and Avenue of the Americas. Or splurge at **Norma's** (in the Parker Meridien at 119 W 56th Street), which serves the city's most expensive breakfast till 3pm.

### Afternoon
Walk east to **Fifth Avenue** (▷ 30–31) and let the shopping spree begin—even if you're just window shopping and ogling the fabulous displays. If you enter only one store, make it **Saks Fifth Avenue** (▷ 125); the perfume and cosmetic counters fill the ground floor. Just north is the beautiful **St. Patrick's Cathedral** (▷ 71).

### Mid-afternoon
Turn east on 45th Street and walk to the Park Avenue entrance of **Grand Central Terminal** (▷ 34–35). Admire its stunning main concourse, then head downstairs for a welcome rest and a snack in the **Dining Concourse** (▷ 145). Exit on 42nd Street, and detour one block east to step into the art deco lobby of the **Chrysler Building** (▷ 67). Then walk west on 42nd Street to Fifth Avenue, and visit the **New York Public Library** (left; ▷ 48–49).

### Evening
As dusk falls, continue west and turn right up Broadway into **Times Square** (▷ 56–57), in all its neon glory. Head for the **TKTS booth** (▷ 56), where you may get a discount ticket for a Broadway show.

### Dinner
Times Square is notorious for chain restaurants, but a good choice for real New York fare is **John's Pizzeria** (▷ 146). There's a branch of **Carmine's** (▷ 144) at 200 W 44th Street, off Times Square.

### Late evening
Afterwards, take in that Broadway show, and/or grab a cab to end the evening with the best nightcap of all: the view of the twinkling lights of Manhattan from the top of the **Empire State Building** (right; ▷ 28–29).

Columbus Circle

Coliseum Park

Time Warner Center

The Pond

5th Avenue/59th Street

59th Street Columbus Circle

Central Park South

9

West 58th St

West 58th Street

Museum of Arts and Design (MAD)

57th Street

WEST 57TH STREET

Carnegie Hall

Parker Meridien Hotel

WEST 57TH STREET

57th Street

Trump Tower

Columbus Avenue

West 56th Street

West 56th Street

MIDTOWN

6th Avenue

West 55th Street

5th Avenue

West 55th Street

Carnegie Deli

West 54th Street

Museum of Modern Art

West 53rd Street

Halal Guys

5th Avenue/53rd Street

7th Avenue

10

West 52nd Street

West 52nd Street

9th Avenue

West 51st Street

West 51st Street

St Patrick's Cathedral

50th Street

West 50th Street

50th Street

49th Street

Radio City Music Hall

'wichcraft, Rock Center Café

8th Avenue

West 49th Street

Rockefeller Center

Saks Fifth Avenue

West 48th Street

47th-50th Streets Rockefeller Ctr

West 48th Street

West 47th Street

THEATER DISTRICT

West 47th Street

West 46th Street

TKTS booth

West 46th Street

Fifth Avenue

11

West 45th Street

Times Square

West 45th Street

West 44th Street

John's

Carmine's

West 44th Street

MIDTOWN

West 43rd Street

42nd Street Port Authority Bus Terminal

Reuters Building

Times Square 42nd Street

West 43rd Street

WEST 42ND STREET

42nd Street Bryant Park

5th Avenue

WEST 42ND STREET

Port Authority Bus Terminal

New Amsterdam Theater

New York Public Library

Bryant Park

West 40th Street

West 40th Street

West 39th Street

West 39th Street

8th Avenue

7th Avenue

Broadway

6th Avenue

West 38th Street

5th Avenue

12

West 38th Street

West 37th Street

GARMENT DISTRICT

West 37th Street

KOREATOWN

9th Avenue

West 36th Street

West 36th Street

West 35th Street

West 35th Street

34th Street Penn Station

Macy's

WEST 34TH STREET

WEST 34TH STREET

34th Street Penn Station

34th Street Herald Square

West 33rd Street

West 33rd Street

Empire State Building

Madison Square Garden

PENN STATION

West 32nd Street

MIDTOWN SOUTH

13

West 31st Street

West 31st Street

West 30th Street

C

West 30th Street

D

West 30th Street

**SIGHTS AND EXPERIENCES**

**Empire State Building (▷ 28)**
The most famous New York sky-scraper affords panoramic views over Manhattan by day or night.

**Fifth Avenue (▷ 30)**
For high fashion, style and quality, there's no better place to shop than Fifth Avenue.

**Grand Central Terminal (▷ 34)**
Some half a million people pass through this stunning Beaux Arts concourse every day.

**Museum of Modern Art (▷ 46)**
From 19th-century masterpieces to contemporary art, this is one of the city's leading museums.

**New York Public Library (▷ 48)**
See the fine carved ceiling and the glorious reading rooms of this Beaux Arts landmark.

**Rockefeller Center (▷ 50)**
Admire the plaza and artworks of this urban complex, then take in the view from the Top of the Rock.

**Times Square (▷ 56)**
Come here at night to see the blitz of neon at the heart of New York's famous Theater District or browse in its megastores by day.

## MORE TO SEE     64

Chrysler Building
Morgan Library & Museum
St. Patrick's Cathedral
Trump Tower
United Nations Headquarters

## SHOP     114

**Clothes**
Brooks Brothers
Dolce and Gabbana
Thomas Pink
**Department Stores**
Bergdorf Goodman
Macy's
Saks Fifth Avenue

**Homewares**
Michael C. Fina
**Shoes**
Manolo Blahnik
**Sports Goods**
Niketown New York
**Technology**
Apple Store

## ENTERTAINMENT     126

**Bars**
Four Seasons Hotel TY Bar
**Classical Music**
Carnegie Hall
**Jazz**
Birdland
**Live Music**
PlayStation Theater
Madison Square Garden

**Theater/Performance**
The New Victory Theater
New World Stages
Radio City Music Hall
Signature Theater
**TV Show Recording**
The Tonight Show

## EAT     138

**Asian**
Kajitsu
**Casual**
Grand Central Terminal
   Dining Concourse
John's Pizzeria
**Classic NY**
'21' Club
Oyster Bar

**Contemporary**
Le Bernardin
Casa Lever
Per Se
**European**
Uncle Nick's

# Upper East Side and Central Park

Central Park is a huge green space accessible to all New Yorkers. The museums of the Upper East Side, facing the park along Fifth Avenue, are renowned worldwide. Their collections range from priceless antiquities to modern art, design, ethnic culture and history.

## Morning
It's unlikely you'll visit more than two museums in a day. This tour will take you past the most popular, and give you a taste of Central Park in between. Most museums don't open until 10am, so start with an early morning stroll in **Central Park** (left; ▷ 18–19). Enter at the southeast corner by Grand Army Plaza (E 59th Street and Fifth Avenue). A pedestrian path (just in from Fifth Avenue) leads to the zoo. If you follow the paved road, first detour to the Pond, with lovely views of the skyline, before reaching the Dairy Visitor Center, where you can pick up a park map. Continue north along The Mall, lined with one of the largest stands of elm trees in America. The southern end, Literary Walk, has statues of famous writers.

## Mid-morning
Just before the Naumburg Bandshell, veer right and follow paths to exit the park at 69th Street. Go one block north to visit the **Frick Collection** (▷ 32–33). Otherwise, continue through the park to the Bethesda Terrace and Fountain (right), overlooking the Lake. Admire the view, then take the pedestrian walkway beneath the terrace—look up to see the Minton tile ceiling, designed by British architect Jacob Wrey Mould. Follow the lakeside path to your right. At Loeb Boathouse veer right to the Conservatory Water, the pretty model boat pond.

## Lunch
The Met, Guggenheim, Cooper Hewitt and Neue Galerie all have cafés. In Central Park, the **Loeb Boathouse** restaurant (▷ 147) has an express café as well as formal dining on the terrace. Alternatively picnic on the Great Lawn behind the Met.

## Afternoon
A visit to the **Metropolitan Museum of Art** (left; ▷ 44–45) is always worthwhile. It stands right in Central Park. Try to catch a free tour of the museum's highlights (times vary). At Fifth Avenue and 86th Street is the **Neue Galerie** (▷ 70). Further north at 89th Street is the **Guggenheim Museum** (▷ 38–39), housed in Frank Lloyd Wright's stunning circular building. Beyond is the **Cooper Hewitt Smithsonian Design Museum** (▷ 22–23) and the **Jewish Museum** (▷ 68). All of these face Central Park's famous Reservoir. The running track and bridle path around the Reservoir are good places to stroll.

## Evening
In summer, Central Park has evening events (Shakespeare in the Park; concerts on the Great Lawn), but be aware of your surroundings when in the park after dark. If a museum has a late night, evenings are a good time to visit and explore, or head for a cocktail at **Bemelmans Bar** (Carlyle Hotel, 35 E 76th Street, tel 212/744-1600).

## Dinner
The superb (and pricey) French cuisine at nearby **Café Boulud** (▷ 143) makes it a good choice for dinner.

## Late evening
Return to Carlyle Hotel's **Café Carlyle** (▷ 132) for jazz and cabaret.

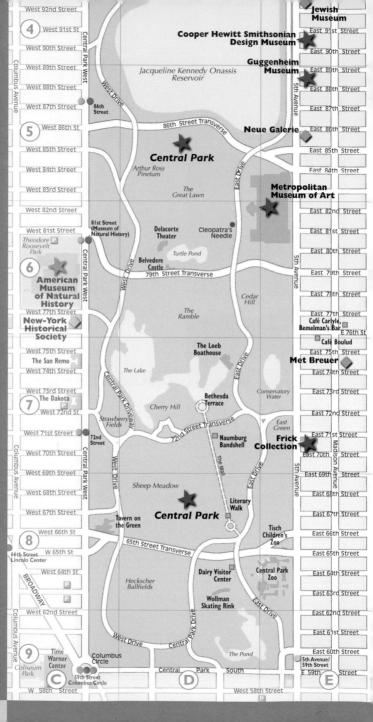

# Upper East Side and Central Park
## Quick Reference Guide

**SIGHTS AND EXPERIENCES**

### Central Park (▷ 18)

This great, green expanse is a visionary creation in the heart of the city. Join New Yorkers as they walk, jog, cycle, row, picnic, stroll with their dogs, play ball and escape the urban buzz.

### Cooper Hewitt Smithsonian Design Museum (▷ 22)

An eclectic mix of old-school and cutting-edge, the superb collections of furniture and decorative arts in the Carnegie mansion are stunning.

### Frick Collection (▷ 32)

The mansion of this 19th-century robber baron is worth a visit in itself, and forms a splendid backdrop for his magnificent collection of old masters and decorative arts.

### Guggenheim Museum (▷ 38)

Frank Lloyd Wright's ground-breaking, nautilus-shaped building with its internal spiral walkway gets all the glory, but the collection of late19th- and 20th-century art is also worth a look.

### Metropolitan Museum of Art (▷ 44)

Don't be daunted by the sheer vastness of this fabulous art museum. Viewing just one or two of its wonderful collections will leave lasting memories.

## MORE TO SEE 64

Jewish Museum
Met Breuer
El Museo del Barrio
Museum of the City of New York
Neue Galerie

## SHOP 114

**Books**
Kitchen Arts and Letters
**Clothes**
Calvin Klein
Ralph Lauren

**Department Stores**
Barneys
Bloomingdale's

## ENTERTAINMENT 126

**Bars**
Auction House
Roof Garden Café and Martini Bar
  at the Met
**Comedy**
Dangerfield's

**Jazz**
Café Carlyle
**Literary Events/Readings**
92nd Street Y
**Theater/Performance**
Florence Gould Hall
Shakespeare in the Park

## EAT 138

**Casual**
Jackson Hole
Serendipity 3
**Classic NY**
Loeb Boathouse
**Contemporary**
Café Boulud
Daniel

**European**
Café Sabarsky
**Middle Eastern**
Persepolis

# Upper West Side

The area west of Central Park is a largely residential, pleasantly leafy neighborhood of grand apartment buildings and big brownstones. Its major attractions are Lincoln Center and the wonderful American Museum of Natural History.

### Morning

Start at **Lincoln Center** (▷ 42–43). Walk around the plaza, admiring the Revson Fountain, the Metropolitan Opera House and other cultural venues. Guided tours are available if you want to go behind the scenes; they leave from the David Rubenstein Atrium. From the northeast corner of the Lincoln Center, cross over the intersection with Broadway to the **American Folk Art Museum** (left; ▷ 66). Continue up Columbus Avenue, taking in its shops and restaurants. If you're ready for a snack, you'll pass the **Magnolia Bakery** (200 Columbus Avenue)—it's never too early for one of their cupcakes.

### Mid-morning

Turn right on W 72nd Street. On the corner with Central Park West is the Dakota, the first luxury co-op apartment building on the Upper West Side. Its most famous resident, former Beatle John Lennon, was fatally shot outside the south gate in 1980. Cross over the road to enter **Central Park** (▷ 18–19), and follow the path to Strawberry Fields, where the black-and-white *Imagine* mosaic (right) is the centerpoint of a peace garden and a memorial to the singer-songwriter. From here there is a good view of the Dakota and the towers of the neighboring San Remo Apartments. Farther on is the **New-York Historical Society** (▷ 71). Cross back to Central Park West and continue on 73rd Street to Broadway.

### Lunch

Broadway is another great shopping street. Continue north to 80th Street, where you can put together a picnic from the gourmet fare at **Zabar's** (right; ▷ 125), or get a sandwich at their adjoining café. Take it to **Riverside Park**, two blocks west, with views over the Hudson River.

### Afternoon

Plan to spend the entire afternoon at the **American Museum of Natural History** (▷ 14–15). Highlights include the dinosaur halls, the animal dioramas, the Rose Center for Earth and Space (left) and more.

### Dinner

You won't have too much further to walk for an early dinner at **Blossom on Columbus** (▷ 143), the uptown outpost of this beloved vegetarian mini-chain, which emphasizes seasonal ingredients.

### Evening

End where you started by retracing your steps back to **Lincoln Center** (right). Even if you haven't got tickets for an evening performance, a walk through the lit-up plaza is a magical way to end the day.

West 92nd Street
West 91st Street
West 90th Street
West 89th Street
West 88th Street
West 87th Street
West 86th Street
West 85th Street
West 84th Street
West 83rd Street
West 82nd Street
West 81st Street
West 80th Street
West 79th Street
West 78th Street
West 77th Street
West 76th Street
West 75th Street
West 74th Street
West 73rd Street
West 72nd Street
West 71st Street
West 70th Street
West 69th Street
West 68th Street
West 67th Street
West 66th Street
West 65th Street
West 64th Street
West 63rd Street
West 62nd Street
West 61st Street
West 60th Street
West 59th Street
West 58th Street

West 72nd Street
West 64th Street
West 63rd Street
West 61st Street

HENRY HUDSON PARKWAY
JOE DIMAGGIO HIGHWAY
Riverside Drive
West End Avenue
BROADWAY
Amsterdam Avenue
Columbus Avenue
Central Park West
Riverside Boulevard
Freedom Place

Riverside Park
Hudson River
Riverside Park

86th Street
86th Street
81st Street (Museum of Natural History)
79th Street
72nd Street
72nd Street
66th Street Lincoln Center
59th Street Columbus Circle

Blossom on Columbus
Zabar's
Theodore Roosevelt Park
American Museum of Natural History
New-York Historical Society
The San Remo
The Dakota
Ansonia Building
UPPER WEST SIDE
Magnolia Bakery
American Folk Art Museum
Juilliard School
Lincoln Center
LINCOLN SQUARE
Damrosch Park
Fordham University Lincoln Center Campus
Time Warner Center
Columbus Circle
Coliseum Park

A    B    C
4    5    6    7    8    9

East 92nd Street

**CARNEGIE HILL**

**Cooper Hewitt Smithsonian**
**Design Museum**

East 91st Street

East 90th street

*Jacqueline Kennedy Onassis*
*Reservoir*

**Guggenheim**
**Museum**

East 89th Street

Park Avenue

Lexington Avenue

3RD AVENUE

East 88th Street

East 87th Street

5th Avenue

East 86th Street

86th Street

**Neue Galerie**

86th Street Transverse

West Drive

East 85th Street

★
**Central Park**

East 84th Street

*Arthur Ross*
*Pinetum*

*The*
*Great Lawn*

East Drive

**Metropolitan**
**Museum of Art**

East 82nd Street

**Delacorte**
**Theater**

**Cleopatra's**
**Needle**

★

East 81st Street

*Turtle Pond*

East 80th Street

**Belvedere**
**Castle**

79th Street Transverse

East 79th Street

East 78th Street

*Cedar*
*Hill*

*The*
*Ramble*

East 77th Street

77th Street

East 76th Street

**The Loeb**
**Boathouse**

East Drive

East 75th Street

*The Lake*

East 74th Street

*Conservatory*
*Water*

East 73rd Street

Central Park Driveway

*Cherry Hill*

East 72nd Street

**UPPER EAST SIDE**

72nd Street Transverse

*East*
*Green*

East 71st Street

*Strawberry*
*Fields*

**Naumburg**
**Bandshell**

**Frick**
**Collection**

★

East 70th Street

**Asia Society**
**and Museum**

Park Avenue

3RD AVENUE

West Drive

*The Mall*

East 69th Street

5th Avenue

Madison Avenue

**Hunter**
**College**

**68th Street**
**Hunter College**

P

East 68th Street

*Sheep Meadow*

East 67th Street

Lexington Avenue

★
**Central Park**

East 66th Street

**Tavern on**
**the Green**

**Tisch**
**Children's**
**Zoo**

East 65th Street

65th Street Transverse

East 64th Street

**Central Park**
**Zoo**

East 63rd Street

**Lexington Avenue/**
**63rd Street**

*Heckscher*
*Ballfields*

**Wollman**
**Skating Rink**

East Drive

East 62nd Street

0          250 m

0          250 yds

East 61st Street

**Lexington Avenue/**
**59th Street**

West Drive

Central Park Drive

East 60th Street

**Central Park South**

*The Pond*

**5th Avenue/**
**59th Street**

**59th Street**

**D**

**E**

East 59th Street

**F**

P

West 58th Street

East 58th Street

P

**SIGHTS AND EXPERIENCES**

### American Museum of Natural History (▷ 14)

This is the largest natural history museum in the world. The lifesize, rearing Barosaurus in the main entrance hall leads to the renowned dinosaur halls, where fossil specimens of some of the earliest dinosaur discoveries are displayed. Add to that a priceless collection of gemstones, animal dioramas, the Rose Center for Earth and Space with its amazing planetarium, and more, and you could easily spend a day here.

### Lincoln Center (▷ 42)

New York's premier performing arts complex is a sight to behold, with its gushing fountains and gleaming buildings, the huge arched windows and chandeliers of the Metropolitan Opera House, and the glowing lights reflected in its wide central plaza. In addition to housing the Metropolitan Opera, it is home to the New York Philharmonic, the Juilliard School of Music, the New York City Ballet and many others, and offers a vast array of entertainment.

*View of Central Park West, including the Dakota and San Remo apartment buildings*

## MORE TO SEE — 64

American Folk Art Museum
Museum of Arts and Design
New-York Historical Society

## SHOP — 114

**Accessories**
Laila Rowe
**Beauty**
Bluemercury Apothecary & Spa
**Clothes**
Malia Mills
Steven Alan

**Food and Wine**
Zabar's
**Sports Goods**
Patagonia

## ENTERTAINMENT — 126

**Bars**
Parkview Lounge
**Cinema**
Lincoln Plaza Cinema
**Classical Music**
David Geffen Hall
Cathedral of St. John
  the Divine
The Metropolitan Opera
**Comedy**
Stand Up NY

**Dance**
David H. Koch Theater
**Jazz**
Dizzy's Club Coca Cola
Smoke
**Live Music**
Beacon Theatre
**Theater/Performance**
Symphony Space

## EAT — 138

**Casual**
Barney Greengrass
Boat Basin Café
**Contemporary**
Blossom on Columbus
Jean-Georges

**Italian**
Carmine's
**Mexican**
Rosa Mexicano

# Farther Afield

New York's outer boroughs are predominantly residential, but that doesn't mean there isn't plenty to see, especially in Brooklyn (▷ 16–17). With an early start, you can take in its top sights as well as two classic New York experiences.

### Morning

Join the morning bustle of the city's commuters and begin your day at the tip of Manhattan at the Staten Island Ferry Terminal. Of course, you'll be heading in the opposite direction, but no matter. The ferry ride (right) across Upper New York Bay is stunning in both directions and, even better, it's free. If you can, ride on the ferry's outside deck to get a good view of the Statue of Liberty—visible from the right side of the boat on the outward journey—and other sights. The round trip to and from **Staten Island** (▷ 75) takes an hour; when you arrive you can catch the next ferry back to Manhattan.

### Mid-morning

Disembark and walk up Broadway to Bowling Green, where you can catch the No. 4 or 5 subway train to the Brooklyn Bridge/City Hall stop. On Park Row, a sidewalk entrance leads up to the wooden walkway of **Brooklyn Bridge** (left; ▷ 66). A walk (or jog) across the bridge is a must, and New Yorkers love it as much as visitors do. It's about a 20-minute walk, though it can take twice as long with stops to admire the views back to the Manhattan skyline.

## Lunch

When you come to the end of the bridge, you'll have worked up an appetite so, when you see the DUMBO sign, take the stairwell down to the street and head towards the water. **Grimaldi's** (▷ 145) on Front Street has some of the best pizza in New York. Afterwards, walk along the promenade for splendid vistas across the river to Manhattan.

## Afternoon

Walk through the pretty brown-stone-lined streets of Brooklyn Heights to the Clark Street subway stop, and take 2 or 3 subway to the Eastern Parkway stop. This eastern side of Prospect Park contains two of Brooklyn's finest attractions: the **Brooklyn Museum of Art** (right; ▷ 16), and **Brooklyn Botanic Garden** (900 Washington Avenue, tel 718/623-7200), with its rose garden, bonsai museum and Japanese Hill-and-Pond Garden. A visit to either could take up the rest of the afternoon.

## Dinner

To get to Williamsburg and **Peter Luger** (▷ 148) for dinner, the quickest route is to take the 2 or 3 subway to Fulton Street in Manhattan and change to the J train to Marcy Ave. If pricey red meat isn't your thing, stroll along Bedford Avenue, which is lined with inexpensive dining options.

## Late evening

Williamsburg is filled with fun bars and live music. A good bet is the **Music Hall of Williamsburg** (66 N Sixth Street, tel 718/486-5400), which draws local talent, internationally known indie rockers, spoken word artists and more. Or venture into neighboring Greenpoint to the **Black Rabbit** (91 Greenpoint Avenue, tel 718/349-1595), a local watering hole with a friendly vibe.

This is a map image showing the New York City and New Jersey metropolitan area.

**NEW JERSEY** cities and towns:
Teaneck, Englewood, Saddle Brook, Hackensack, Bogota, Garfield, Hasbrouck Heights, Ridgefield Park, Palisades Park, Fort Lee, Passaic, Clifton, Wallington, Moonachie, Ridgefield, Fairview, Nutley, Rutherford, Secaucus, West New York, Weehawken, Belleville, North Arlington, Union City, Kearny, Hoboken, Harrison, Newark, Jersey City, Bayonne, Lyndhurst

**NEW YORK**:
HARLEM, NEW YORK, MANHATTAN, Central Park, Brooklyn, Brooklyn Museum of Art, Prospect Park, Brooklyn Botanic Gardens, BOROUGH PARK, GRAVESEND, STATEN ISLAND, PORT RICHMOND, CLIFTON, ARROCHAR, LIGHTHOUSE HILL, GREAT KILLS, Coney Island

Landmarks and features:
George Washington Bridge, Henry Hudson Parkway, Palisades Interstate Parkway, Hudson River, Hackensack River, East River, Lincoln Tunnel, Holland Tunnel, Queensboro Bridge, Manhattan Bridge, Brooklyn Bridge, Hugh L. Carey Tunnel, Governors Island, Ellis Island, Statue of Liberty, Liberty State Park, Newark Liberty International Airport, Verrazano Narrows Bridge, Bayonne Bridge, Upper New York Bay, Lower New York Bay, Newark Bay, Gateway National Recreation Area, LaTourette Park, FDR Drive, Belt Parkway, Ocean Parkway, Prospect Expy, New Jersey Turnpike (Eastern Spur, Western Spur), Garden State Parkway

Roads: 80, 46, 21, 3, 17, 95, 9, 280, 440, 78, 1, 9A, 495, 27, 19, 20

Street references: 125th St, 57th St, 34th St, 14th St, 2nd Ave

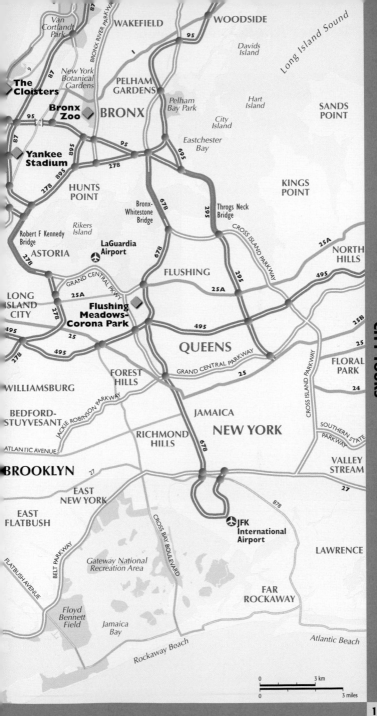

# Farther Afield Quick Reference Guide

## SIGHTS AND EXPERIENCES

### Brooklyn (▷ 16–17)

If you've ever wondered what New York is like beyond Manhattan, Brooklyn is the best place to start. Brooklyn Heights is lined with classic brownstones. The Brooklyn Museum of Art contains a renowned Egyptian collection and the Sackler Center for Feminist Art. Alongside is the Brooklyn Botanic Garden. Walk back to Manhattan across the Brooklyn Bridge—a classic New York experience. Williamsburg, with its trendy boutiques and bars, is lively on evenings and weekends.

| MORE TO SEE | 64 |
|---|---|

Bronx Zoo
The Cloisters
Coney Island
Flushing Meadows–Corona Park
Harlem
Staten Island
Yankee Stadium

| EAT | 138 |
|---|---|

**Casual**
Grimaldi's
**Classic NY**
Peter Luger

**Contemporary**
Blue Ribbon Brasserie
Henry's End
River Café

1920
THE WONDER WHEEL,
A 150 FOOT TALL FERRIS WHEEL
OPENS AT CONEY ISLAND.

# Shop

**Whether you're looking for the best local products, a department store or a quirky boutique, you'll find them all in New York. In this section shops are listed alphabetically.**

| | |
|---|---|
| Introduction | **116** |
| Directory | **118** |
| Shopping A–Z | **119** |

SHOP

# Introduction

Thought there was nothing you couldn't buy over the internet? Think again. New York is a shopping heaven, with clothing, furniture, food and souvenirs available no place else. Shopping is still one of the best ways to get an inside look at life in New York—its trends, pace, cultural influences and sense of humor. From massive department stores to small boutiques, the city has something for everyone.

### One of a Kind
New York has seen a boom in artisanal and unique producers in the last decade, from chocolatiers to distilleries to jewelers. Keep an eye out for trunk shows, pop-up stores, and craft fairs where makers sell their wares.

### Fashion
For fashion head for Nolita and SoHo, where small (and often expensive) boutiques line the streets. Major franchises can also be found here, along Broadway, and side streets such as Prince Street, Broome Street and Spring Street. For the most upscale fashion choices, head to Madison Avenue north of 59th Street, where the smartest New York shops all have outposts.

### Music
Although the growth of downloads has seen the demise of many of the large music retailers, there is still much to delight the

---

**WINDOW SHOPPING**

Start on Lexington between 59th and 60th streets and you'll see the flags outside Bloomingdale's. Walk west to Madison Avenue; between 60th and 61st streets is Barney's, for expensive clothing, jewelry, accessories and beauty products. Walk west along 57th Street, past Chanel and Christian Dior, to Bergdorf Goodman. On Fifth Avenue peer in at Gucci, Tiffany's and Henri Bendel.

---

*Clockwise from top: A store on Fifth Avenue; a T-shirt that says it all; pretzels to go; looking for a bargain at*

enthusiast. The city's branches of Academy Records boast collections of vintage classical and rock vinyl and used CDs; Bleecker Street Records and House of Oldies are prime browsing spots in Greenwich Village; or check out the Metropolitan Opera Shop (metoperashop.org) for something a little more classical. Note that most American DVDs cannot be played on European machines.

## Bargains

If you're looking for a bargain, try the popular sample sales, where designer brands are marked down as much as 80 percent. Designer sales are often held at open show-rooms over a few days. Arrive early on the first day of the sale for the best selection, though prices do drop as days go by. To find out about upcoming sales and shopping trends pick up *New York* magazine or *Time Out New York*.

## A Bite to Eat

NYC is known for noshing: hot dogs, a slice of pizza, a bagel with a schmear or street food from mobile food vendors. These range from Middle Eastern falafel carts to waffle stands and vegan lunch trucks. A handy guide to locating a gourmet food truck around town is nyctruckfood.com, which automatically updates.

### FLEA MARKETS

You can find everything from silver and beaded jewelry to clothing, artworks and antiques at the Brooklyn Flea (brooklynflea.com), which in warm weather is in Williamsburg and in winter months moves to Industry City (check website for details). Uptown, check out the huge GreenFlea market on Sunday (✉ Columbus Avenue between 76th and 77th streets ⏰ 10–5.30). In good weather, weekend street fairs pop up in different neighborhoods. Check newyorkled.com/nyc_events_street_fairs.htm for a comprehensive schedule.

*the Brooklyn Flea Market; don't miss the Midtown department stores; a boutique in Greenwich Village*

# Directory

## Lower Manhattan

**Books**
The Mysterious Bookshop
**Clothes**
Abercrombie & Fitch
Resurrection
**Discount**
Century 21
**Food and Wine**
The Pickle Guys
**Homewares**
New Kam Man
**Shoes**
Alife Rivington Club

## Downtown and Chelsea

**Accessories**
Village Tannery
**Beauty**
C.O. Bigelow
Kiehl's
**Books**
Barnes & Noble
Strand
**Clothes**
Cynthia Rowley
Hotoveli
Jeffrey New York
Kenneth Cole
Marc Jacobs
Scoop
**Food and Wine**
Chelsea Market
Eataly
Union Square Greenmarket
**Homewares**
ABC Carpet and Home
**Shoes**
DSW
**Toys**
Kidding Around

## Midtown

**Clothes**
Brooks Brothers
Dolce & Gabbana
Thomas Pink
**Department Stores**
Bergdorf Goodman
Macy's
Saks Fifth Avenue
**Homewares**
Michael C. Fina
**Shoes**
Manolo Blahnik
**Sports Goods**
Niketown New York
**Technology**
Apple Store

## Upper East Side and Central Park

**Books**
Kitchen Arts and Letters
**Clothes**
Calvin Klein
Ralph Lauren
**Department Stores**
Barneys
Bloomingdale's

## Upper West Side

**Accessories**
Laila Rowe
**Beauty**
Bluemercury Apothecary & Spa
**Clothes**
Malia Mills
Steven Alan
**Food and Wine**
Zabar's
**Sports Goods**
Patagonia

SHOP

# Shopping A-Z

### ABC CARPET AND HOME
abchome.com
Here are seven floors of extremely carefully edited homewares, from four-poster beds to handkerchiefs to artisinal lotions. The shared esthetic mixes mid-19th-century design museum, Venetian palace and deluxe hotel.
➕ E15 ✉ 888 Broadway/E 19th Street ☎ 212/473-3000 Ⓜ 4, 5, 6, N, Q, R 14th Street–Union Square

### ABERCROMBIE & FITCH
abercrombie.com
Teens and college grads are the core customers at this temple to slouchy American style, famous for its rather racy Bruce Weber-shot catalogs. The clothes, though, are perfect for anyone's weekends and the prices are gentle. There are men's and women's lines.
➕ F21 ✉ 199 Water Street/Fulton Street ☎ 212/809-9000 Ⓜ 2, 3, 4, 5, A, C, J, Z Fulton Street–Broadway–Nassau

### ALIFE RIVINGTON CLUB
alifenewyork.com
Here, behind an unmarked door, sneakers are high fashion, with all the latest footwear from American,

European and Japanese brands. Great colors and limited editions are available.
➕ G18 ✉ 158 Rivington Street, between Clinton and Suffolk streets ☎ 212/432-7200 Ⓜ F, J, Z Delancey Street–Essex Street

### APPLE STORE
apple.com
This 24-hour-a-day, 365-day-a-year showcase store is certain to delight ingrained Mac-geeks as well as those in thrall to Apple's industry-leading design and stylish simplicity. Stores can also be found in the Meatpacking District, SoHo, and the Upper West Side.
➕ E9 ✉ 767 5th Avenue/59th Street ☎ 212/336-1440 Ⓜ N, R 5th Avenue–59th Street

### BARNES & NOBLE
barnesandnoble.com
The flagship B&N has the widest new book selection in the city. Check the website for upcoming evening readings and regular author book signing events.
➕ E15 ✉ 33 E 17th Street ☎ 212/253-0810 Ⓜ 4, 5, 6, N, Q, R, L 14th Street–Union Square

*The iconic 24-hour Apple Store on Fifth Avenue*

*A New York institution*

## BARNEYS

barneys.com

Some New Yorkers source their entire wardrobe from this high-fashion store. Ranging over several floors are avant-garde designers, the store's own-label clothes, high-end cosmetics, great menswear, an epic shoe department, jewelry, homewares, kids' clothes and more. Prices are high.

✚ E9 ✉ 660 Madison Avenue/61st Street ☎ 212/826-8900 🚇 N, R 5th Avenue–59th Street

## BERGDORF GOODMAN

bergdorfgoodman.com

For the most refined shopping experience in New York, the eight-floor fashion-for-lunching-ladies department store on the site of a Vanderbilt mansion takes the cake.

✚ E9 ✉ 754 5th Avenue/58th Street ☎ 800/558-1855 🚇 N, R 5th Avenue–59th Street

## BLOOMINGDALE'S

bloomingdales.com

Bloomingdale's opened in 1879 and is one of the most venerable names in Manhattan, yet it keeps up with the latest trends. Great for jewelry and handbags.

✚ F9 ✉ Lexington/59th Street ☎ 212/705-2000 🚇 4, 5, 6, F, N, R 59th Street

## BLUEMERCURY APOTHECARY & SPA

bluemercury.com

From top brand cosmetics to spa treatments, hair care, famous fragrances and gorgeous candles, Bluemercury is a welcome addition to the Upper West Side retail experience.

✚ B5 ✉ 2305 Broadway/83rd Street ☎ 212/799-0500 🚇 1 86th Street

## BROOKS BROTHERS

brooksbrothers.com

Home of the preppy, Brooks Brothers also caters to anyone, male or female, who wants to look pulled together (though the men's department is far better). Their basics, like boxer shorts and white dress shirts, are exceptional.

✚ E11 ✉ 346 Madison Avenue/44th Street ☎ 212/682-8800 🚇 4, 5, 6, 7, S Grand Central

---

### THE SHOPS AT COLUMBUS CIRCLE

The closest thing to a mall in Manhattan, The Shops at Columbus Circle in the Time Warner Center has reclaimed Columbus Circle from the traffic. The stores are on the lowest four levels (restaurants above). The *pièce de résistance* is the Whole Foods Market.
✚ C9 ✉ Time Warner Center, Broadway (59th/60th Street) ☎ 212/823-6300, shopsatcolumbuscircle.com 🚇 A, B, C, D, 1 59th Street–Columbus Circle

## CALVIN KLEIN

calvinklein.com

The iconic New York designer's flagship store, designed by John Pawson, is as minimal as his clothing, without even racks to spoil the clean lines (you simply point at a display and request your size). His homeware collection is downstairs.

🗺 E9  ✉ 654 Madison Avenue/60th Street  ☎ 212/292-9000  🚇 N, R 5th Avenue–59th Street

## CENTURY 21

c21stores.com

Practically a cult, Century 21 sells discounted chic womenswear, especially by European designers.

🗺 E21  ✉ 22 Cortlandt Street between Church Street and Broadway  ☎ 212/227-9092  🚇 4, 5 Fulton Street

## CHELSEA MARKET

chelseamarket.com

More than a store, this enormous former Nabisco factory has an array of unique of food boutiques, bakeries, cafés, coffee shops and delis under one roof. Even if you're not hungry, it's enjoyable to stroll through for the architect-honed warehouse and inhale the mouth-watering aromas.

🗺 C15  ✉ 75 9th Avenue/15th Street  ☎ 212/652-2110  🚇 A, C, E, L 14th Street

## C.O. BIGELOW

bigelowchemists.com

The oldest apothecary in America (est. 1838) offers a wide range of products for pampering yourself from head to toe. In addition to well-known international brands, the store also has its own line, which includes everything from lotions to candles.

🗺 D16  ✉ 414 Sixth Avenue/9th Street  ☎ 212/533-2700  🚇 A, C, E, B, D, F, M West 4th Street

## CYNTHIA ROWLEY

cynthiarowley.com

Shop here for adorable, chic dresses, separates and shoes. There's also a sports and swimwear collection—check out the striking wetsuits.

🗺 C16  ✉ 376 Bleecker Street (between Perry and Charles streets)  ☎ 212/242-3803  🚇 1 Christopher Street–Sheridan Square

## DOLCE & GABBANA

dolcegabbana.com

This is the flagship New York store for cutting-edge styles from fashion's dynamic duo.

🗺 E9  ✉ 717 5th Avenue/55th Street  ☎ 212/897-9653  🚇 N, R 5th Avenue E, M 5th Avenue–53rd Street

## DSW

dsw.com

DSW stands for "Designer Shoe Warehouse," with Prada, Kate Spade, Via Spiga and other designer names at discounted prices. Choose from women's trendy heels and pumps, sandals and beachwear; men's; children's; sports shoes; handbags and more. Other branches in Midtown and the Upper West Side.

🗺 E15  ✉ 40 E 14th Street, Union Square South at University Place  ☎ 212/674-2146  🚇 L, N, Q, R, 4, 5, 6 Union Square

## EATALY

eataly.com/nyc

Offering a cornucopia of fresh and packaged Italian foodstuffs from coffee to gelato to housemade pastas, Eataly is as close as one can come to a real Italian food bazaar. There are also a dozen places to grab a bite.

⊞ D14 ✉ 200 5th Avenue/23rd Street
☎ 212/229-2560 🚇 N, R 23rd Street

## HOTOVELI

hotoveli.com

Chic French and Italian creations dominate in this stylish West Village emporium.

⊞ C16 ✉ 271 W 4th Street, between Perry and W 11th streets ☎ 212/206-7722
🚇 1 Christopher Street–Sheridan Square

## JEFFREY NEW YORK

jeffreynewyork.com

One of the coolest places in the Meatpacking District, this compact department store has a resident DJ, a spacious all-white interior and non-pushy assistants. It all makes for a pleasant visit—and an expensive one if you fall for the wares.

⊞ B15 ✉ 449 W 14th Street/9th–10th avenues ☎ 212/206-1272 🚇 A, C, E, L 14th Street

## KENNETH COLE

kennethcole.com

Don't be fooled by the minimalist design of the clothier's flagship store: If what you are looking for isn't on display, the shop's high-tech digital touchscreens showcase the full line and the store will deliver same-day in the city.

⊞ F17 ✉ 328 Bowery/Bond Street
☎ 212/777-2013 🚇 6 Bleecker Street

## KIDDING AROUND

kiddingaroundtoys.com

From newborns to teens, everyone will find something to their taste at this toy emporium, which stocks everything from popular board-games to hard-to-find children's musical instruments.

⊞ E15 ✉ 60 W 15th Street/Avenue of the Americas ☎ 212/645-6337 🚇 F, M 14th Street, L 6th Avenue

## KIEHL'S

kiehls.com

High-end face and body products, made from naturally derived ingredients, are sold in upscale black-and-white packaging. The store has been an East Village fixture since 1851—the pear tree out front commemorates one that was planted by Dutch colonial governor Peter Stuyvesant.

⊞ F15 ✉ 109 3rd Avenue/13th Street
☎ 212/677-3171 🚇 L 3rd Avenue

## KITCHEN ARTS AND LETTERS

kitchenartsandletters.com

Specializing in food and drink, this independent bookstore stocks the latest bestsellers, as well as classics from leading authors like James Beard and Julia Child. The knowledgable staff can also source rare and out-of-print titles for you.

⊞ E4 ✉ 1435 Lexington Avenue, between 93rd and 94th streets ☎ 212/876-5550
🚇 6 96th Street

### SINGULAR SOUVENIRS

Anyone can bring home an "I Love NY" T-shirt. For more upscale gifts, try museum gift shops. The Metroplitan Museum (▷ 44–45) and MoMA (▷ 46–47) are well stocked and the Lower East Side Tenement Museum (▷ 68) has the best selection of NYC-themed books. Prefer to nosh? The Pickle Guys (▷ 124) ships across the USA. Or check out the New York City Transit Museum shop at Grand Central Terminal for unique gifts—subway token cufflinks, anyone?

### LAILA ROWE

lailarowe.com

This is one of a growing chain-ette of accessories stores, crammed with colorful gear. Expect a fun vibe and selections of jewelry at prices that won't break the bank.

➕ C7 ✉ 493 Columbus Avenue/84th Street ☎ 212/724-2680 🚇 B, C, 1 86th Street

### MACY'S

macys.com

The sign outside says it's the largest store in the world, and by the time you've explored all 11 levels of this huge department store, you'll believe it.

➕ D12 ✉ 151 W 34th Street/Herald Square ☎ 212/695-4400 🚇 B, D, F, N, R 34th Street

### MALIA MILLS

maliamills.com

This swimwear emporium is cherished by every woman who fears her reflection. There are mix-and-match pieces made to fit everyone, in super-cool designs.

➕ C7 ✉ 220 Columbus Avenue/70th Street ☎ 212/874-7200 🚇 1, 2, 3, B, C 72nd Street

### MANOLO BLAHNIK

manoloblahnik.com

Come here for beautifully made shoes by one of the world's great shoe designers.

➕ D10 ✉ 31 W 54th Street ☎ 212/582-3007 🚇 E, M 5th Avenue–53rd Street

### MARC JACOBS

marcjacobs.com

Fashion's favorite darling, Marc Jacobs put once-Bohemian Bleecker Street on the retail map.

➕ C16 ✉ 403-405 Bleecker Street/ W 11th Street ☎ 212/924-0026 🚇 1, 2 Christopher Street–Sheridan Square

### MICHAEL C. FINA

michaelcfina.com

This very exclusive purveyor of gifts and tableware is *the* place for wedding lists.

➕ E9 ✉ 500 Park Avenue/E 59th Street ☎ 800/289-3462 🚇 4, 5, 6, 7 Grand Central

### THE MYSTERIOUS BOOKSHOP

mysteriousbookshop.com

This is a must for crime and mystery lovers. Staff will lead you to new discoveries alongside

*The largest store in the world*

writers such as Patricia Highsmith and Raymond Chandler. Rare books are available.

➕ E20  ✉ 58 Warren Street between Church Street and West Broadway ☎ 212/587-1011 🚇 1, 2, 3, A, C, E Chambers Street

### NEW KAM MAN

newkamman.com

This Chinatown shop calls itself a "destination for all things Asian," and it's easy to see why. From home decor to herbal remedies to take-out food, there's a little bit of everything here.

➕ F19  ✉ 200 Canal Street/Mulberry Street ☎ 212/571-0330 🚇 6, N, Q, J, Z Canal Street

### NIKETOWN NEW YORK

nike.com

You can feel like a professional athlete here as you browse the latest sportswear. Expect high-tech videos and multilevel displays in an industrial atmosphere.

➕ D9  ✉ 6 E 57th Street, between 5th and Madison avenues ☎ 212/891-6453 🚇 N, R 57th Street

For great designer vintage head for Resurrection on Mott Street

### PATAGONIA

patagonia.com

If you like environmental consciousness with your outdoor wear but still want to look slick while climbing the mountain, or just look like you might have done so, this is your place.

➕ C6  ✉ 426 Columbus Avenue/81st Street ☎ 917/441-0011 🚇 B, C 81st Street–Museum of Natural History

### THE PICKLE GUYS

thepickleguys.com

Carrying on a Lower East Side tradition, the Pickle Guys still brine the old-fashioned way, selling pickles, olives, pickled watermelon (in season) and more out of barrels in their small storefront, much as it might have been done a century ago.

➕ G19  ✉ 49 Essex Street/Grand Street ☎ 212/656-9739 🚇 F Delancey Street, J, Z Essex Street

### RALPH LAUREN

ralphlauren.com

Distinguished cowboy and English country heritage looks are sold out of the Rhinelander Mansion, a turn-of-the-20th-century house.

➕ E7  ✉ 867 Madison Avenue, between E 71st and 72nd streets ☎ 212/606-2100 🚇 6 68th Street–Hunter College

### RESURRECTION

resurrectionvintage.com

You'll find a haul of pricey but perfect vintage, with an emphasis on collectible labels: Pucci, Halston, Courrèges, Dior. The owners offer their own line of skirts and tops.

➕ F18  ✉ 217 Mott Street, between Spring and Prince streets ☎ 212/625-1374 🚇 6 Spring Street

## SAKS FIFTH AVENUE

saksfifthavenue.com

Found on the famous street with the same name, this is the flagship store of the now nationwide chain, with a fabulous range of designer fashions for men and women.

🔳 E10 ✉ 611 5th Avenue/49th–50th streets ☎ 212/753-4000 🚇 E, F 5th Avenue

## SCOOP

scoopnyc.com

Well-known designers (Helmut Lang, Zac Posen) sit alongside Scoop's in-house brand.

🔳 B15 ✉ 861 Washington Street/W 13th Street ☎ 212/691-1905 🚇 A, C, E 14th Street

## STEVEN ALAN

stevenalan.com

A Lower East Side look on the Upper West Side, this is a carefully edited array of cutting-edge labels, some of them available nowhere else—including Alan's own designs.

🔳 B5 ✉ 465 Amsterdam Avenue/82nd Street ☎ 212/595-8451 🚇 1, 2, 3, 79th Street–Broadway; A, C, E 81st Street–Central Park West

## STRAND

strandbooks.com

Filled with 18 miles (30km) of new and used books, this fabulous bookstore is a New York City institution. From popular and hot-off-the-presses bestsellers to antique volumes purchased from estate sales, the Strand has something for everyone. The New York City section is particularly strong.

🔳 E16 ✉ 828 Broadway/12th Street ☎ 212/473-1452 🚇 4, 5, 6, N, Q, R, L 14th Street–Union Square

### GREAT GREENMARKET

On four days a week (🚇 Mon, Wed, Fri, Sat 8–6) Union Square is home to the city's biggest and best greenmarket (grownyc.org/greenmarket). An entire culture has grown around this collection of stalls overflowing with homegrown and homemade produce from farms in the tri-state area. Favorites include maple candies, Amish cheeses and New York honey from rooftop beehives.

## THOMAS PINK

thomaspink.com

Beautifully tailored shirts for men and women line the shelves of the New York outlet of this classic British label.

🔳 E10 ✉ 520 Madison Avenue/E 53rd Street ☎ 212/838-1928 🚇 E, M 5th Avenue–53rd Street

## VILLAGE TANNERY

villagetannery.com

Love leather? Look no further—stylish leather goods, designed by artisan Sevestet, made to order and handcrafted from the finest materials can be found here. There are handbags, briefcases, backpacks, belts and more to choose from.

🔳 D17 ✉ 173 Bleecker Street ☎ 212/673-5444 🚇 A, C, E, B, D, F, M West 4th Street–Washington Square

## ZABAR'S

zabars.com

This foodie haven has a Jewish soul all its own. Cheese, coffee, smoked fish and the like are downstairs, while upstairs showcases the city's best buys in kitchenwares.

🔳 B6 ✉ 2245 Broadway/80th Street ☎ 212/787-2000 🚇 1 79th Street

SHOP

125

# Entertainment

**Once you're done with sightseeing for the day, you'll find lots of other great things to do with your time in this chapter, even if all you want to do is relax with a drink. In this section establishments are listed alphabetically.**

Introduction                    128
Directory                       130
Entertainment A–Z               131

ENTERTAINMENT

# Introduction

As the sun sets over New York, the city becomes a sultry, romantic and mysterious place. For spectacular sunset views, stroll along the pedestrian path on the banks of the Hudson River on the West Side, then wander through Times Square as the bright billboards pop out from the dark sky.

### Nightlife

As young New Yorkers explore new frontiers in the city, the Meatpacking District—once known for drugs and prostitution—has become home to trendy bars and clubs. Celebrity sightings are common at Spice Market (403 W 13th Street, tel 212/675-2322) and Cielo (18 Little West 12th Street, tel 212/645-5700). At the other end of the spectrum are neighborhood joints like the Ear Inn (326 Spring Street at Washington Street (tel 212/226-9060) and Fat Cat Billiards (75 Christopher Street in West Village, tel 212/675-6056), friendly dives where the beer flows cheaply and the music is loud.

A short stroll away, a string of music bars sit cheek by jowl along two blocks of Bleecker Street between LaGuardia Place and Sullivan Street, including the venerable folk-rock haven, The Bitter End (147 Bleecker Street, tel 212/673-7030), still going strong after more than 50 years. Around the corner is Café Wha? (▷ 132), where Dylan and Hendrix once played, and now a dance club.

---

**FOR A LAUGH**

Comedy clubs are a great way to sample New York's sense of humor. Venues such as Caroline's (✉ 1626 Broadway, at 50th Street ☎ 212/757-4100, carolines.com), Upright Citizens Brigade Theatre (✉ 307 W 26th Street, between 8th and 9th avenues ☎ 212/366-9176, ucbtheatre.com), Stand Up NY (▷ 137) and Gotham (▷ 134) are popular. At many clubs, you'll see a mix of established acts and rising stars.

*Clockwise from top: Blue Note in Greenwich Village is one of the best places for jazz; the old Paramount Theater, Times Square; Alice Tully Hall, Lincoln Center;*

Another hot nightlife neighborhood is the Lower East Side, where there's a raft of rock 'n' roll bars fanning out from Ludlow and Stanton streets. Leading the pack are Arlene's Grocery (▷ 131), Pianos (158 Ludlow Street, tel 212/505-3733) and Rockwood Music Hall (196 Allen Street, tel 212/477-4155).

### Broadway and Beyond
Top Broadway shows can be expensive, but you can pick up some great bargains at the TKTS booth in Times Square and other locations (tdf.org/tkts). Off-Broadway venues are less expensive and you might just catch the next big hit on its way up. A night at Lincoln Center (▷ 42–43) is an unforgettable New York experience, whether you opt for a production at the Metropolitan Opera (▷ 135), a symphony at David Geffen Hall (▷ 131), a ballet at the David H. Koch Theater, or one of the more intimate venues.

### Take to the Water
Circle Line Cruises' evening boat rides around Manhattan are a relaxing and memorable way to experience the world's most famous skyline. Board at Pier 83, at 42nd Street on the Hudson River (tel 212/563-3200). Tour guides on board relate the legends of the city (circleline42.com).

## LIVE MUSIC

Rock bands perform at Bowery Ballroom (✉ 6 Delancey Street, boweryballroom.com) and Irving Plaza (✉ 17 Irving Plaza, irvingplaza.com), while Madison Square Garden (▷ 134) hosts blockbuster tours. You can hear everything from classical music to pop at Carnegie Hall (▷ 132). Among the top jazz clubs are Blue Note (▷ 132) and Village Vanguard (✉ 178 7th Avenue South, villagevanguard.com) in Greenwich Village, and Iridium in Midtown (✉ 1650 Broadway, theiridium.com).

*Gotham Comedy Club; a quiet table à deux in the Meatpacking District; take to the water to see the New York skyline by night*

**ENTERTAINMENT**

# Directory

## Lower Manhattan

**Bars**
The Dead Rabbit Grocery and Grog
Parkside Lounge
The Porterhouse at Fraunces Tavern
Wassail
**Cinema**
Film Forum
**Clubs**
Arlene's Grocery
Beach at Governors Island
SOB's
**Comedy**
Comedy Cellar
**Live Music**
City Winery

## Downtown and Chelsea

**Bars**
McSorley's Old Ale House
Pete's Tavern
White Horse Tavern
**Cabaret**
Joe's Pub
**Clubs**
Café Wha?
**Comedy**
Gotham Comedy Club
**Jazz**
Blue Note
**Karaoke**
Sing Sing Karaoke
**Live Music**
Mercury Lounge
**Theater/Performance**
Cherry Lane Theatre

## Midtown

**Bars**
Four Seasons Hotel TY Bar
**Classical Music**
Carnegie Hall
**Jazz**
Birdland
**Live Music**
Madison Square Garden
PlayStation Theater

**Theater/Performance**
The New Victory Theater
New World Stages
Radio City Music Hall
Signature Theatre
**TV Show Recording**
The Tonight Show
    starring Jimmy Fallon

## Upper East Side and Central Park

**Bars**
Auction House
Parkview Lounge
Roof Garden Café and Martini Bar
    at the Met
**Comedy**
Dangerfield's
**Jazz**
Café Carlyle
**Literary Events/Readings**
92nd Street Y
**Theater/Performance**
Florence Gould Hall
Shakespeare in the Park

## Upper West Side

**Cinema**
Lincoln Plaza Cinema
**Classical Music**
David Geffen Hall
Cathedral of St. John the Divine
The Metropolitan Opera
**Comedy**
Stand Up NY
**Dance**
David H. Koch Theater
**Jazz**
Dizzy's Club Coca Cola
Smoke
**Live Music**
Beacon Theatre
**Theater/Performance**
Symphony Space

ENTERTAINMENT

# Entertainment A–Z

## 92ND STREET Y

92Y.org

A varied program of events is held here including readings by renowned authors, folk music, jazz and lectures on a range of subjects.

🔲 E4 ✉ 1395 Lexington Avenue/92nd Street ☎ 212/415-5500 🚇 6 96th Street

## ARLENE'S GROCERY

arlenesgrocery.net

This is one of the best rock clubs in the city, where hot new bands make their name.

🔲 G18 ✉ 95 Stanton Street, between Ludlow and Orchard streets ☎ 212/358-1633 🚇 F, M 2nd Avenue

## AUCTION HOUSE

With sumptouous red velvet drapes, a fireplace, sofas and candlelight, this is more suited to a romantic drink than a rowdy night out. The no-furs, no-sneakers dress code gives an idea of the casual-chic ambience.

🔲 F4 ✉ 300 E 89th Street/Second Avenue ☎ 212/427-4458 🚇 4, 5, 6 86th Street

## BEACH AT GOVERNORS ISLAND

governorsbeachclub.com

This summer venue for live events with bars, a café and beer garden has views of the Manhattan skyline as you boogie to DJs and big-name bands.

🔲 Off map ✉ Governors Island ☎ 212/896-4600 ⛴ Ferry from Battery

*Check out the cocktails*

Maritime Building Slip at 10 South Street 🚇 1 South Ferry, R Whiteall

## BEACON THEATRE

beacontheatre.com

The Beacon is one of the premier venues in the city, featuring multi-night stands by established artists such as Bob Dylan and Tom Petty, as well as many rising stars.

🔲 B7 ✉ 2124 Broadway/74th Street ☎ 212/465-6500 🚇 1, 2, 3 72nd Street

## BIRDLAND

birdlandjazz.com

Big names, big bands, John Coltrane tributes and Cubans are the rage here. The club was established in New York in 1949.

🔲 C11 ✉ 315 W 44th Street/8th–9th avenues ☎ 212/581-3080 🚇 A, C, E 42nd Street–Port Authority Bus Terminal

---

### COCKTAIL CULTURE

Cocktail culture is alive and well in the Big Apple. The Martini craze is here to stay—many lounges and bars offer long menus of creative concoctions. Elegant glassware is crucial. Atmospheres range from urban chic to clubby lounge to pubs. Neighborhood pubs, with more emphasis on beer and bourbon, are favorite watering holes. Or, instead of going for alcohol, visit one of New York's coffee bars.

*Carnegie Hall*

## BLUE NOTE

bluenote.net

Jazz artists from around the world play two shows nightly at this popular Village jazz club and restaurant.

🔲 D17 ✉ 131 W 3rd Street/6th Avenue–MacDougal Street ☎ 212/475-8592 🚇 A, C, E, B, D, F 4th Street–Washington Square

## CAFÉ CARLYLE

thecarlyle.com

This lounge in the elegant Carlyle Hotel was home to the great Bobby Short until his death in 2005, but his spirit lives on in the piano players, lounge singers and jazz bands. Be sure to look in at Bemelmans Bar, with its whimsical murals of Central Park by the artist Ludwig Bemelmans.

🔲 E6 ✉ 35 E 76th Street, Madison Avenue ☎ 212/744-1600 🚇 6 77th Street

## CAFÉ WHA?

cafewha.com

In business since the 1950s, this has been a hot spot ever since Bob Dylan and Jimi Hendrix used to hang out here. The Boss started his career here. It's still going strong, with bands performing nightly and styles ranging from R&B to soul and modern rock.

🔲 D17 ✉ 115 MacDougal Street/Minetta Lane ☎ 212/254-3706 🚇 A, B, C, D, E, F, M 4th Street–Washington Square

## CARNEGIE HALL

carnegiehall.org

This world-class recital hall features an eclectic program from classical artists to folk singers, world music and pop. With so much choice, you are bound to find a concert that appeals to you.

🔲 D9 ✉ 881 7th Avenue/57th Street ☎ 212/247-7800 🚇 N, R 57th Street; E 7th Avenue

## CATHEDRAL OF ST. JOHN THE DIVINE

stjohndivine.org

The cathedral provides a varied program of liturgical, cultural and civic events.

🔲 B1 ✉ 1047 Amsterdam Avenue/112th Street ☎ 212/316-7540 🚇 1 Cathedral Parkway–110th Street

## CHERRY LANE THEATRE

cherrylanetheatre.org

This historic theater in Greenwich Village presents a vibrant program of landmark plays and works by emerging playwrights.

🔲 C17 ✉ 38 Commerce Street between Barrow and Bedford streets ☎ 212/989-2020 🚇 1 Christopher Street–Sheridan Square

## CITY WINERY

citywinery.com/newyork

Events from intimate evenings with singer-songwriters to gourmet cooking demonstrations take place here. It's a fully functioning winery, too, with tastings and a shop.

➕ D18 ✉ 155 Varick Street/Vandam Street ☎ 212/608-0555 🚇 C, E Spring Street; 1 Houston

## COMEDY CELLAR

comedycellar.com
A cozy Greenwich Village spot, this attracts well-known comedians from time to time. The intimate nature of the venue means you are quite likely to find you are part of the show, so be warned.

➕ D17 ✉ 117 MacDougal Street, between W 3rd Street and Minetta Lane and 130 W 3rd Street ☎ 212/254-3480 🚇 A, B, C, D, E, F, M 4th Street–Washington Square

## DANGERFIELD'S

dangerfields.com
This comedy club, established in 1969, is still going strong with claims to be the oldest in the world. Those who have performed here include Jay Leno and Jim Carrey.

➕ F9 ✉ 1118 1st Avenue/61st Street ☎ 212/593-1650 🚇 4, 5, 6 59th Street

## DAVID GEFFEN HALL

lincolncenter.org
In 2015, mogul David Geffen donated $100 million to rename and revamp concert venue Avery Fisher Hall, home to the New York Philharmonic.

➕ B8 ✉ 10 Lincoln Center Plaza, Columbus Avenue/65th Street ☎ 212/875-5030 🚇 1 66th Street–Lincoln Center

## DAVID H. KOCH THEATER

davidhkochtheater.com
nycballet.com
This sumptuous auditorium is the home of the New York City Ballet, which performs here September through June.

➕ B8 ✉ 20 Lincoln Center Plaza at 63rd Street ☎ 212/496-0600 🚇 1 66th Street–Lincoln Center

## THE DEAD RABBIT GROCERY AND GROG

deadrabbitnyc.com
Every drink on the Dead Rabbit's extensive upstairs menu is historically sourced, giving patrons a flavor of old New York.

➕ E23 ✉ 30 Water Street/Broad Street ☎ 646/422-7906 🚇 1 South Ferry, R Whitehall

## DIZZY'S CLUB COCA COLA

jazz.org/dizzys
Jazz at Lincoln Center's intimate club is—in the spirit of Dizzy Gillespie—designed to ensure that performers and spectators alike relaaaaax. There are After Hours sets Tuesday through Saturday.

➕ C9 ✉ Time Warner Center at Broadway/60th Street, 5th floor ☎ 212/258-9595 🚇 A, B, C, D, 1 59th Street–Columbus Circle

## FILM FORUM

filmforum.com
New York's best revival house shows everything from silent films (with live accompaniment) to

---

### KEEPING UP

One of New York's favorite pastimes is keeping up with what's on. Look for extensive weekly listings in the magazines *New York*, *Time Out New York* and *The New Yorker*, or the Friday and Sunday editions of the *New York Times*. You can also pick up free copies of the *Village Voice* and *New York Press* newspapers in storefronts and vestibules around town. The monthly listings in *Paper* magazine have a decidedly downtown focus.

independent movie premieres, documentaries and classics.

➕ D18 ✉ 209 W Houston Street/Varick Street ☎ 212/727-8110 🚇 1 Houston Street

## FLORENCE GOULD HALL

fiaf.org

Associated with the Alliance Française, this concert hall stages music, dance, jazz and readings with a French theme.

➕ E9 ✉ 55 E 59th Street/Park–Madison avenues ☎ 212/355-6160 🚇 N, R 5th Avenue–59th Street

## FOUR SEASONS HOTEL TY BAR

fourseasons.com/newyork

I.M. Pei design, a smooth vibe and a great Martini menu make the TY lobby bar an excellent choice for cocktails.

➕ E9 ✉ 57 E 57th Street/Madison Avenue ☎ 212/758-5700 🚇 4, 5, 6 Lexington Avenue–59th Street

## GOTHAM COMEDY CLUB

gothamcomedyclub.com

Gotham showcases top stars as well as up-and-coming comedians.

➕ C14 ✉ 208 W 23rd Street/7th Avenue ☎ 212/367-9000 🚇 N, R, 1 23rd Street; F, Path 23rd Street

## JOE'S PUB

joespub.com

Known for its sound quality, the performance space here always has an interesting line-up of singers, comedians, magicians and burlesque artists.

➕ E16 ✉ The Public Theater, 425 Lafayette Street/Astor Place ☎ 212/967-7555 🚇 N, R 8th Street–NYU; 6 Astor Place

## LINCOLN PLAZA CINEMA

lincolnplazacinema.com

Several screens show successful first runs and also foreign movies.

➕ B8 ✉ 1886 Broadway/63rd Street ☎ 212/757-2280 🚇 1 66th Street–Lincoln Center

## MADISON SQUARE GARDEN

thegarden.com

The giant concrete circle is one of the city's major venues for music and sporting events. For the box office enter the Main Ticket Lobby at 7th Avenue and 32nd Street.

➕ C13 ✉ 4 Pennsylvania Plaza ☎ 212/465-6741 🚇 1, 2, 3 34th Street–Penn Station

## MCSORLEY'S OLD ALE HOUSE

New York's oldest saloon (1854) draws a crowd with its sawdust-covered floors, coal-burning stove and working-class history.

➕ F16 ✉ 15 E 7th Street/3rd Avenue ☎ 212/473-9148 🚇 6 Astor Place

## MERCURY LOUNGE

mercuryloungenyc.com

Its laid-back atmosphere attracts eclectic performers.

## CABARET

The term has undergone so many image overhauls, it's now settled into being a catch-all for entertainment options ranging from off-Broadway cabaret theater and downtown crooners sitting around the piano bar at Duplex (✉ 61 Christopher Street ☎ 212/255-5438, theduplex.com) to the Broadway supper club at 54 Below (☎ 254 W 54th Street, ☎ 646/476-3551, 54below.com). Joe's Pub (above) is among the venues that offer what you might call classic, though modernized, cabaret.

New York's late-night scene ranges from all-night parties to more staid amusements. The Meatpacking District is home to many popular spots, including sister clubs Le Bain (444 W 13th Street, tel 212/645-7600), with its rooftop hot tubs, and Top of the Standard (848 Washington Street), atop the High Line. At the Landmark Sunshine Cinema (143 E Houston Street, tel 212/260-7289), weekend midnight movies mix classics and cult favorites.

✚ F17  ✉ 217 E Houston Street/Essex Street  ☎ 212/260-4700  🚇 F 2nd Avenue

## THE METROPOLITAN OPERA

metopera.org

The gala openings at this world-class opera house rank among the most glamorous of the city's cultural events. Visit the website at noon for same day rush tickets. The box office is at the north end of the front lobby. The season runs from October to April.

✚ B8  ✉ 30 Lincoln Center  ☎ 212/362-6000  🚇 1 66th Street–Lincoln Center

## THE NEW VICTORY THEATER

newvictory.org

If you have kids (five or older) in tow, there'll be something here to thrill them and keep them entertained.

✚ C11  ✉ 209 W 42nd Street/7th–8th avenues  ☎ 646/223-3010  🚇 1, 2, 3, 7, N, R, Q Times Square–42nd Street

## NEW WORLD STAGES

newworldstages.com

Check out the top off-Broadway productions, from musicals to kids' shows, at this state-of-the-art theatrical venue.

✚ C10  ✉ 340 W 50th Street/8th Avenue  ☎ 646/871-1730  🚇 C, E 50th Street

## PARKSIDE LOUNGE

parksidelounge.net

Parkside hosts live music, stand-up and karaoke, as well as people just having a beer. It's open until 4am, and is a relaxed and unpretentious place.

✚ G17  ✉ 317 E Houston Street/Attorney Street  ☎ 212/673-6270  🚇 F, M 2nd Avenue

## PARKVIEW LOUNGE

parkviewloungenyc.com

Enjoy impressively designed surroundings, fine food and drink, and stunning views of Central Park and Broadway.

✚ C9  ✉ Time Warner Center, Columbus Circle  ☎ 212/823-9770  🚇 A, B, C, D 59th Street–Columbus Circle

## PETE'S TAVERN

petestavern.com

A favorite with locals, this fine 1864 Gramercy Park Victorian saloon has a welcoming feel.

✚ E15  ✉ 129 E 18th Street/Irving Place  ☎ 212/473-7676  🚇 L, N, R, 4, 6 14th Street–Union Square

One of the best reasons to brave the summer heat in New York is for the wonderful choice of free entertainment put on by many of the city's premier cultural institutions. Without paying a dime it's possible to enjoy alfresco operas, theater, art, eating, jazz, classical music, movies, dance, rock-and-roll, blues and folk music. Many people arrive early for performances by popular artists and stake out a good spot for a picnic.

**ENTERTAINMENT**

**OUT IN CENTRAL PARK**

Central Park is a welcoming park. For those who crave physical activity there's lots to do.
*Bike Riding* You can rent a no-frills bicycle.
*Rowing* Rent rowboats from the Loeb Boathouse and venture out on the Lake.
*Ice Skating* Wollman Rink rents skates in winter and becomes an amusement park in summer.
*Running* The park is the most popular place for running and jogging.

### PLAYSTATION THEATER

playstationtheater.com
This theater is a medium-size venue for medium-big acts in a great location in the center of Times Square.
🚇 C11/D11 ✉ 1515 Broadway/44th Street ☎ 212/930-1950 🚇 1, 2, 3, 7, N, Q, R, S Times Square–42nd Street

### THE PORTERHOUSE AT FRAUNCES TAVERN

frauncestavern.com
This 18th-century watering hole, where George Washington bade goodbye to his officers after the Revolutionary War, is now the first stateside branch of Dublin's Porterhouse Brewing Company. It has fine ales and a restaurant.
🚇 E22 ✉ 54 Pearl Street/Broad Street ☎ 212/968-1776 🚇 N, R Whitehall Street

*Famous since the 1930s*

### RADIO CITY MUSIC HALL

radiocity.com
This landmark art deco theater, which opened in 1932, hosts several music shows a year. You can also take an hour-long tour.
🚇 D10 ✉ 1260 6th Avenue/50th Street ☎ 212/247-4777 🕐 Varied; tours daily 10–5 🚇 B, D, F, M 40th–50th streets–Rockefeller Center

### ROOF GARDEN CAFÉ AND MARTINI BAR AT THE MET

metmuseum.org
You can get cocktails and simple food on this rooftop terrace dotted with sculpture. Use the elevator in the European Sculpture and Decorative Arts galleries. The café is open May through late fall.
🚇 D5 ✉ Metropolitan Museum of Art, 1000 5th Avenue/82nd Street ☎ 212/535-7710 🚇 6 86th Street

### SHAKESPEARE IN THE PARK

publictheater.org
The Shakespeare festival is a high-light of summer in Central Park. Line up for free tickets as soon as possible, or chance your luck with virtual ticketing.
🚇 C6 ✉ Delacorte Theater in Central Park, 81st Street (west side) ☎ 212/539-8500 🚇 B, C 81st Street

### SIGNATURE THEATRE

signaturetheatre.org
Every season at this off-Broadway house, designed by Frank Gehry,

has a new playwright-in-residence from the first ranks of American theater. Even if you are not here for a show, you can enjoy the café/bar in the upstairs lobby.

🏢 B11 ✉ 480 W 42nd Street/10th Avenue ☎ 2212/244-7529 🚇 A, C, E 42nd Street

## SING SING KARAOKE
karaokesingsing.com
You'll be able to sing your heart out in this popular karaoke venue.

🏢 G17 ✉ 81 Avenue A/E 5th and 6th Street ☎ 212/674-0700 🚇 F, M Lower East Side–2nd Avenue

## SMOKE
smokejazz.com
Plush couches adorn this intimate jazz lounge, which hosts local and well-known names.

🏢 B2 ✉ 2751 Broadway/106th Street ☎ 212/864-6662 🚇 1 103rd Street

## SOB'S
sobs.com
The Latin beat keeps you dancing at the tropically themed nightclub Sounds of Brazil. Hear African, reggae and other island music.

🏢 D18 ✉ 204 Varick Street/Houston Street ☎ 212/243-4940 🚇 1 Houston Street

## STAND UP NY
standupny.com
Aspiring comics try out their new routines in this traditional comedy club.

🏢 B6 ✉ 236 W 78th Street/Broadway ☎ 212/595-0850 🚇 1 79th Street

## SYMPHONY SPACE
symphonyspace.org
Head here for storytelling, readings, children's theater, music, dance, film and more.

🏢 B4 ✉ 2537 Broadway/95th Street ☎ 212/864-5400 🚇 1, 2, 3 96th Street

## THE TONIGHT SHOW STARRING JIMMY FALLON
nbc.com/the-tonight-show
Upon taking the helm of *The Tonight Show*, Jimmy Fallon moved it back to New York City for the first time in decades. Take your chance at same-day standby tickets by lining up before 9am on 49th Street across from *The Today Show*.

🏢 D10 ✉ 30 Rockefeller Plaza/49th Street ☎ 212/664-3056 🚇 B, D, F, M 47th–50th Streets–Rockefeller Center

## WASSAIL
wassailnyc.com
Home to 90-plus domestic and imported ciders on tap and in bottles, this bar has taken the Lower East Side by storm. It also serves seasonal vegetarian food.

🏢 G18 ✉ 162 Orchard Street/Stanton Street ☎ 646/918-6835 🚇 F 2nd Avenue

## WHITE HORSE TAVERN
This sprawling 1880s bar was the last watering hole of Welsh poet Dylan Thomas.

🏢 C16 ✉ 567 Hudson Street/11th Street ☎ 212/989-3956 🚇 1 Christopher Street–Sheridan Square

### BIG IN NEW YORK
From the elegance of a grand opera to the excitement of avant-garde performance art, New York spectacles are world-class (even the flops). Broadway shows can be expensive, but nothing transports audiences like a great multimillion-dollar musical or an intense performance by a drama diva. Be sure to reserve tickets in advance for the most popular shows.

# Eat

**There are places to eat across the city to suit all tastes and budgets. In this section establishments are listed alphabetically.**

Introduction                          **140**
Directory                             **141**
Eating A–Z                            **142**

EAT

139

# Introduction

From basic diners serving trademark large portions to über-trendy chefs and chic restaurants showcasing world cuisine, New York really can claim to offer something to suit every taste, diet and budget.

## Around the World

In this global melting pot it's almost impossible not to find just about every cuisine in the world. The city hosts an abundance of celebrity chefs, but also hole-in-the-wall eateries featuring almost every imaginable cuisine. To get a flavor of the city's culinary heritage check out a food tour such as the one offered by Foods of NY tours (foodsofny.com).

## A Day's Dining

No one does breakfast or brunch like Manhattanites (especially on weekends) so make for Greenwich Village or SoHo, grab a copy of the *New York Times* and just chill over your choice of eggs, pancakes or waffles and limitless coffee. For lunch, try a Jewish deli for plenty of atmosphere and gargantuan sandwiches; make for the Dining Concourse on the lower level of Grand Central Terminal (▷ 145); or, if you're downtown, Chinatown or Little Italy should help keep you fueled for the rest of the day's shopping or sightseeing. Dinner in New York can be as casual or as stylish as your mood and budget dictate.

From top: Pancakes with maple syrup in a New York diner; the city has some great pizzerias; Café Boulud, a top restaurant; cheeseburger with fries

---

### TAXES, TIPPING AND FINANCIAL MATTERS

A sales tax of 8.875 percent will be added to your dining bill. The minimum tip (with good service) is 15 percent; people often double the tax for a 17.75 percent tip. Many restaurants offer fixed-price menus, which are good value. Watch for New York Restaurant Week, held twice a year in winter and summer. This special promotion offers a three-course menu at reduced rates for lunch and dinner at many restaurants; this deal is often extended so it's always worth checking if it's available.

EAT

# Directory

## Lower Manhattan

**Asian**
Mission Chinese
Nobu
Vegetarian Dim Sum
**Casual**
The Bailey Pub & Brasserie
Bubby's
Delicatessen
Schillers
**Classic NY**
Katz's Deli
Odeon

## Downtown and Chelsea

**Asian**
Fatty Crab
Ssäm Bar
**Contemporary**
Eleven Madison Park
Gotham Bar and Grill
North Square
The Spotted Pig
**French/American**
Almond
**Italian**
Del Posto
**Polish/Ukrainian**
Veselka

## Midtown

**Asian**
Kajitsu
**Casual**
Grand Central Terminal Dining
    Concourse (▷ panel, 145)
John's Pizzeria
**Classic NY**
'21' Club
Oyster Bar
**Contemporary**
Le Bernardin
Casa Lever
Per Se
**European**
Uncle Nick's

## Upper East Side and Central Park

**Casual**
Jackson Hole
Serendipity 3
**Classic NY**
Loeb Boathouse
**Contemporary**
Café Boulud
Daniel
**European**
Café Sabarsky
**Middle Eastern**
Persepolis

## Upper West Side

**Casual**
Barney Greengrass
Boat Basin Café
**Contemporary**
Blossom on Columbus
Jean-Georges
**Italian**
Carmine's
**Mexican**
Rosa Mexicano

## Farther Afield

**Casual**
Grimaldi's
**Classic NY**
Peter Luger
**Contemporary**
Blue Ribbon Brasserie
Grocery
Henry's End
River Café

EAT

# Eating A-Z

## PRICES

Prices are approximate, based on a 3-course meal for one person.

| | |
|---|---|
| $$$ | over $60 |
| $$ | $40–$60 |
| $ | under $40 |

## '21' CLUB $$$

21club.com

With a history spanning more than eight decades, this eatery doffs a cap to its speakeasy days. Choose from fixed-price menus or an extensive à la carte featuring lobster, steak, salmon and much more. The '21' burger is a perennial favorite.

✚ D10 ✉ 21 W 52nd Street/5th–6th avenues ☎ 212/582-7200 ⏲ Mon–Fri lunch, Mon–Sat dinner ⛿ B, D, F, M 47th–50th streets–Rockefeller Center

## ALMOND $$

almondrestaurant.com

This warm and friendly American bistro uses the freshest ingredients from farm to table. The sea scallops are not to be missed, and it seems a shame to have to share the apple cinnamon crisp for two. Reservations are essential.

✚ E14 ✉ 12 E 22nd Street/Broadway–Park Avenue ☎ 212/228-7557 ⏲ Daily lunch and dinner, weekend brunch ⛿ R 23rd Street

## THE BAILEY PUB & BRASSERIE $–$$

thebaileynyc.com

Just off Wall Street, this is a big hit with the Financial District crowd. The bar, which stays open until 1am, serves British pub-style food. The Brasserie offers excellent yet inexpensive meals, from salads and sandwiches through to steaks and a *plat du jour*.

✚ E22 ✉ 52 William Street ☎ 212/859-2200 ⏲ Daily breakfast, lunch and dinner, weekend brunch ⛿ 2, 3, 4, 5 Wall Street

## BARNEY GREENGRASS $

barneygreengrass.com

An Upper West Side tradition since 1929, this is frantic on weekends, when locals feast on huge platters of smoked fish—whitefish, sable, sturgeon and lox—or have the same ingredients packed into a hearty sandwich.

✚ B5 ✉ 541 Amsterdam Avenue/86th Street ☎ 212/724-4707 ⏲ Tue–Fri 8.30–4, Sat–Sun 8.30–5 ⛿ 1 86th Street

## LE BERNARDIN $$$

le-bernardin.com

Frenchman Eric Ripert is acknowledged to be the fish maestro. Exquisite, inventive dishes are served by super-attentive waiters.

✚ D10 ✉ 155 W 51st Street/7th Avenue ☎ 212/554-1515 ⏲ Mon–Fri lunch, Mon–Sat dinner ⛿ B, D, F, M 47th–50th streets–Rockefeller Center

## FOOD HALLS

Curated, gourmet food halls are all the rage, where diners can select from a variety of different cuisines. In addition to Eataly (▷ 121), check out the Pennsy at Penn Startion (✉ 2 Pennsylvania Plaza), The Todd English Food Hall in lower level of the Plaza Hotel (✉ 1 West 59th Street ☎ 212/986-9260) and Urbanspace Vanderbilt, outside Grand Central (✉ Corner of Vanderbilt Avenue/45th Street ☎ 646/747-0822), home to a constantly changing line-up of concept outlets.

## BLOSSOM ON COLUMBUS $$

blossomnyc.com

This cozy branch of the Blossom empire boasts a selection of biodynamic beers and wines, and top vegetarian fare. The soy bacon cheeseburger has a devoted following—even among omnivores.

➕ C5 ✉ 507 Columbus Avenue/84th Street ☎ 212/875-2600 🕐 Daily lunch and dinner, weekend brunch 🚇 B, C 81st Street–Museum of Natural History

## BLUE RIBBON BRASSERIE $$

blueribbonrestaurants.com

There's a Manhattan feel to this huge modern-American favorite in Brooklyn, and that's not surprising, since it has an older sister there (97 Sullivan Street/Prince Street), liked by off-duty chefs. It combines creative and comfort food.

➕ See map ▷ 111 ✉ 280 5th Avenue/1st Street, Brooklyn ☎ 718/840-0404 🕐 Daily dinner 🚇 R Union Street

## BOAT BASIN CAFÉ $

boatbasincafe.com

It's hard to find this café serving diner-style food on the banks of the Hudson but, if you do, sit at a terrace table. The view is dazzling.

➕ A6 ✉ W 79th Street/Hudson River ☎ 212/496-5542 🕐 Late Mar–Oct (weather permitting) daily lunch and dinner 🚇 1 79th Street

## BUBBY'S $

bubbys.com

A Tribeca favorite, Bubby's serves all-American BLTs, chicken clubs, meat loaf and fries, followed by pies (for example chocolate or peanut butter). Expect a wait for the popular weekend brunch.

➕ D19 ✉ 120 Hudson Street ☎ 212/219-0666 🕐 Daily brunch, dinner 🚇 1, 9 Franklin Street; A, C, E Canal Street

## CAFÉ BOULUD $$–$$$

cafeboulud.com

This Daniel Boulud restaurant has classical, seasonal and ethnic influences. You will find *pot au feu*, *bouillabaisse* and entrées inspired by Spain, Morocco and Vietnam.

➕ E6 ✉ 20 E 76th Street/5th–Madison avenues ☎ 212/772-2600 🕐 Daily breakfast, lunch, dinner, Sun brunch 🚇 6 77th Street

**EAT**

*Bubby's in Tribeca is a favorite choice for weekend brunch*

EAT

## CAFÉ SABARSKY $–$$
neuegallerie.org
The restaurant in the Neue Galerie has premier Austrian chef Kurt Gutenbrunner at the helm. You can also drop in for coffee and cake.
✚ E5 ✉ 1048 5th Avenue/86th Street ☎ 212/288-0665 🕘 Mon, Wed 9–6, Thu–Sun 9–9 🚇 4, 5, 6 86th Street

## CARMINE'S $$
carminesnyc.com
This beloved, raucous place serves Sicilian-Italian dishes family-style—huge platters to share. It's not for picky foodies, but it's fun.
✚ B4 ✉ 2450 Broadway/90th Street ☎ 212/362-2200 🕘 Daily lunch and dinner 🚇 1, 2, 3 96th Street–Broadway

## CASA LEVER $$–$$$
casalever.com
The ocean liner-esque design is the star at this restaurant, downstairs in the Lever House building on Park Avenue, but it would be worth visiting just for chef Mario Danieli's contemporary twists on northern Italian classics.
✚ E10 ✉ 390 Park Avenue/53rd Street ☎ 212/888-2700 🕘 Mon–Fri breakfast, lunch and dinner, Sat brunch and dinner 🚇 E, M Lexington Avenue–53rd Street; 6 51st Street

## DANIEL $$$
danielnyc.com
This formal restaurant serves exquisitely restrained, modern French dishes—opt for the six-course tasting menu to appreciate fully chef Daniel Boulud's brilliance. Dessert arrives with its own basket of warm madeleines.
✚ E8 ✉ 60 E 65th Street/Madison–Park avenues ☎ 212/288-0033 🕘 Mon–Sat dinner 🚇 6 68th Street–Hunter College

## DEL POSTO $$$
delposto.com
Mario Batali, New York's roundly ebullient TV-friendly patron saint of interesting Italian food, may be known for creating rustic dishes in a casual ambience, but this is a swanky, deco-looking, big-night-out restaurant, with piano player, tableside preparations and valet parking. It works beautifully.
✚ B15 ✉ 85 10th Avenue/16th Street ☎ 212/497-8090 🕘 Mon–Fri lunch and dinner, Sat–Sun dinner 🚇 A, C, E, L 14th Street

## DELICATESSEN $
delicatessennyc.com
In need of some comfort food? At this funky SoHo restaurant you can start with cheeseburger spring rolls then finish off with s'mores.
✚ D18 ✉ 54 Prince Street/Lafayette Street ☎ 212/226-0211 🕘 Daily lunch and dinner 🚇 N, R Prince Street

## ELEVEN MADISON PARK $$$
elevenmadisonpark.com
This is one of the world's finest restaurants—and probably the best

---

### VEGGIE DELIGHTS
With a third of Americans now opting to eat vegetarian at least once a week, New York has become a center for creative meat-free restaurants. At the higher end are Kajitsu (▷ 146) and Blossom on Columbus (▷ 143), but veggie lovers should also seek out Peacefood Café (✉ 460 Amsterdam Avenue/82nd Street ☎ 212/362-2266) and celebrity chef Chloe Coscarelli's By Chloe (✉ 185 Bleecker Street/MacDougal Street ☎ 212/290-8000).

in New York. Chef Daniel Humm delivers knockout tasting menus at stratospheric prices. Reserve well in advance.

✚ E14 ✉ 11 Madison Avenue/24th Street ☎ 212/889-0905 ⏱ Daily dinner, Thu–Sat lunch 🚇 6, R 23rd Street

## FATTY CRAB $$

fattycrab.com

Malaysia meets Manhattan in this unpretentious place. It's not just seafood—the short ribs rendang is extremely good. Great wines and cocktails complement the cuisine.

✚ C16 ✉ 643 Hudson Street, between Horatio and Gansevoort ☎ 212/352-3592 ⏱ Daily lunch and dinner 🚇 1, 2, 3 14th Street

## GOTHAM BAR AND GRILL $$$

gothambarandgrill.com

This light and airy restaurant epitomizes New York grandeur, with world-class dishes such as miso-marinated black cod.

✚ E16 ✉ 12 E 12th Street/5th Avenue ☎ 212/620-4020 ⏱ Mon–Fri lunch and dinner, Sat–Sun dinner only 🚇 L, N, R, Q, 4, 5, 6 14th Street–Union Square

## GRIMALDI'S $

grimaldis.com

With one of the few coal brick-ovens left in the city, Grimaldi's pizza restaurant dates back to 1905. Constant lines are testament to its reputation. Credit cards are not accepted.

✚ H21 ✉ 1 Front Street (under Brooklyn Bridge) ☎ 718/858-4300 ⏱ Daily lunch, dinner 🚇 A, C High Street; 2, 3 Clark Street

## HENRY'S END $$

henrysend.com

This neighborhood favorite in Brooklyn has high ceilings, brick

> ### GRAND CENTRAL
>
> Here are some highlights at the Dining Concourse at Grand Central Terminal:
> *Central Market NY* makes creative sandwiches.
> *Café Spice* for curries.
> *Junior's* is a great diner with peerless cheesecake.
> *Magnolia Bakery* for scrumptious pastries.
> *Shake Shack* has world-renowned burgers.
> *Mendy's Kosher Delicatessen* does knishes and pastrami-on-rye.

walls and an open kitchen. The menu features seasonal fish and locally sourced meat and produce, but the highlight is the Wild Game Festival (winter to spring), plus an award-winning wine list.

✚ H22 ✉ 44 Henry Street/Cranberry Street, Brooklyn Heights ☎ 718/834-1776 ⏱ Daily dinner 🚇 A, C High Street; 2, 3 Clark Street

## JACKSON HOLE $

jacksonholeburgers.com

This small chain of burger places is useful when all you want is a hefty

*Sensational sushi*

*A deli to die for*

sandwich in a child-friendly,
no-frills environment.
➕ F8 ✉ 232 E 64th Street/2nd Avenue
☎ 212/371-7187 🕐 Daily breakfast, lunch
and dinner 🚇 6 68th Street–Hunter
College

### JEAN-GEORGES $$$
jean-georges.com
One of the world's great chefs,
Alsace native Jean-Georges
Vongerichten is known for his
refined, full-flavored Asian-
accented cooking. The glass-walled
minimalist rooms feel serene and
special. Lunch here is a (relative)
bargain. Don't miss the molten-
center chocolate cake.
➕ C9 ✉ 1 Central Park West/60th Street
☎ 212/299-3900 🕐 Mon–Sat lunch and
dinner 🚇 A, C, B, D 1 59th Street–
Columbus Circle

### JOHN'S PIZZERIA $
johnspizzerianyc.com
This converted church has one of
just a handful of coal brick-ovens
left in the city. It's a great spot
to head to for a pre- or post-
theater pizza.
➕ C11 ✉ 260 W 44th Street ☎ 212/
391-7560 🕐 Daily lunch and dinner
🚇 1, 2, 3, 7, N, Q, R Times Square–
42nd Street

### KAJITSU $$$
kajitsunyc.com
The only vegetarian restaurant
in New York to be awarded a
Michelin star, Kajitsu promotes
Japanese shojin cuisine through its
multi-course tasting menus. The
choices change each month, with
emphasis on seasonal delights.
Reserve well in advance.
➕ E12 ✉ 129 E 39th Street/Lexington
Avenue ☎ 212/228-4873 🕐 Tue–Sun
dinner 🚇 4, 5, 6, 7, S 42nd Street–Grand
Central

### KATZ'S DELI $
katzsdelicatessen.com
The site of the hilarious climactic
scene in *When Harry Met Sally* is
the last deli in a once thriving
Jewish neighborhood. Opened
in 1888, it upholds traditions such

## NEW YORK RESTAURANT WEEK

The best dining deal in town is no longer a mere seven-day affair. New York Restaurant
Week now takes place twice a year, and lasts for up to a month each winter and summer.
Participating restaurants offer three-course lunches and dinners at a set price. The cost of
your drinks, tax and tip are extra. This event offers a great chance to dine at some of New
York's best and hottest restaurants for a fraction of the normal price. The menus are
designed to show off their classic dishes and cooking styles. Check out the dates and
restaurants at nycgo.com, and book ahead—the best tables go fast!

as plain surroundings, and knishes and pastrami sandwiches.

🔢 G17  ✉ 205 E Houston Street/Ludlow Street  ☎ 212/254-2246  ⏰ Daily breakfast, lunch and dinner  🚇 F, M Lower East Side–2nd Avenue

## LOEB BOATHOUSE $$

thecentralparkboathouse.com

Leave hectic Manhattan behind at this lakeside place in Central Park. The food is contemporary American but the view is the main reason for coming. The cocktail deck gets busy in summer. Reservations are advised.

🔢 D7  ✉ Central Park, nearest to E 72nd Street entrance  ☎ 212/517-2233  ⏰ Mon–Fri lunch and dinner, Sat–Sun brunch and dinner, lunch only Dec–Mar  🚇 6 68th Street–Hunter College

## MISSION CHINESE $$$

mcfny.com

Award-winning chef Danny Bowien's Mission Chinese opened its first NYC branch in 2012. Its current home came with a built-in pizza oven, so Bowien added the Italian staple to his menu of mostly northern Chinese cuisine. Reservations accepted online only.

🔢 G19  ✉ 171 East Broadway/Essex Street  ☎ 212/529-8800  ⏰ Daily dinner, Sat–Sun dim sum brunch  🚇 F East Broadway, J, M, Z Essex Street

## NOBU $$$

noburestaurants.com

It is difficult to get a reservation at this Japanese shrine, part owned by Robert de Niro, but you'll be rewarded by the memorable food and gorgeous, light wood setting. Choose the lobster with wasabi pepper sauce or fresh yellowtail sashimi with jalapeno.

### BRUNCH

It's hard to imagine what New Yorkers did before the invention of brunch. These days the weekend noontime meal can be everything from a basic omelet to a multi-course culinary adventure, and it needn't be consumed before noon. A 2pm brunch with mimosas is just fine.

🔢 D19  ✉ 105 Hudson Street/Franklin Street  ☎ 212/219-0500  ⏰ Mon–Fri lunch and dinner, Sat–Sun dinner only  🚇 1 Franklin Street

## NORTH SQUARE $$

northsquareny.com

Chef Yoel Cruz's inventive cooking focuses on Mediterranean dishes. The atmosphere is relaxed, and dishes such as coriander-crusted yellowfin tuna are sublime. The Sunday jazz brunch has featured Norah Jones, who used to wait tables here.

🔢 D16  ✉ 103 Waverly Place/MacDougal Street  ☎ 212/254-1200  ⏰ Mon–Fri breakfast, lunch and dinner, Sat–Sun brunch and dinner  🚇 A, C, E, B, D, F, M West 4th Street–Washington Square

## ODEON $$

theodeonrestaurant.com

After celebrating its quarter-century in 2005 with all the 80s faces that made it the first hot spot of the Bright Lights, Big City age, this art deco-style restaurant is still going strong. Its tiled floors, dim lighting, happy bar area and open-most-hours welcome are some reasons why—that and the always-reliable nouvelle American cooking.

🔢 D20  ✉ 145 West Broadway/Thomas Street  ☎ 212/233-0507  ⏰ Mon–Fri breakfast, lunch and dinner, Sat–Sun brunch and dinner  🚇 A, C Chambers Street

**EAT**

## OYSTER BAR $$

oysterbarny.com

Some reports suggest this 1913 vaulted room in Grand Central Terminal may be resting on past glories, but for a thoroughly New York experience it's hard to beat.

⊞ E11 ✉ Grand Central Terminal, lower level ☎ 212/490-6650 🕐 Mon–Sat lunch and dinner 🚇 4, 5, 6, 7 Grand Central–42nd Street

## PER SE $$$

perseny.com

If you want to know what all the fuss is about, reserve *way* ahead for Thomas Keller's idiosyncratic cuisine, such as smoked river sturgeon with violet artichokes, peas and mint cream. Enjoy great views from the window tables.

⊞ C9 ✉ Time Warner Center, 10 Columbus Circle, 4th floor/60th Street ☎ 212/823-9335 🕐 Daily dinner, Fri–Sun lunch 🚇 A, C, B, D, 1 59th Street–Columbus Circle

## PERSEPOLIS $$

persepolisnewyork.com

Thai chef San Sethachutkul took to Persian cooking with great flair when he came to New York, serving some of the city's finest Middle Eastern cuisine. Try the delicious saffron-marinated rack of lamb.

⊞ F7 ✉ 1407 Second Avenue/73rd Street ☎ 212/535-1100 🕐 Daily lunch and dinner 🚇 6 68th Street–Hunter College

## PETER LUGER $$$

peterluger.com

This unpretentious steakhouse has been serving the city's best beef to hungry New Yorkers since 1887. No need for embellishment, simply order hash browns and creamed spinach to accompany your steak. Reserve early. No credit cards.

⊞ See map ▷ 111 ✉ 178 Broadway/Driggs Avenue, Brooklyn ☎ 718/387-7400 🕐 Daily lunch and dinner 🚇 J, Z Marcy Avenue

## RIVER CAFÉ $$$

rivercafe.com

For a special occasion (jackets required, guys) and drop-dead views across the East River to Manhattan, this is a treat. Classic international food ranges from caviar and wild rock lobster to rabbit and dumplings.

⊞ See map ▷ 111 ✉ 1 Water Street (under the Brooklyn Bridge) ☎ 718/522-5200 🕐 Mon–Sat lunch and dinner, Sun brunch and dinner 🚇 A, C High Street; 2, 3 Clark Street

## ROSA MEXICANO $$

rosamexicano.com

A favorite among Lincoln Center theater-goers, Rosa Mexicano's menu offers traditional Mexican cooking, while the David Rockwell-designed interior—including a 30ft (9m) blue-tiled wall of water—is totally contemporary.

### FOOD ON WHEELS

The lowly hot dog stand and pretzel cart have stepped up a notch. More than 3,000 gourmet food trucks now ply the streets of Manhattan, serving up a variety of tasty, healthy and inexpensive fare to busy New Yorkers on the go. Doling out everything from biryanis to Korean BBQ, organic salads to schnitzel and Belgian waffles, some have reached near-cult status. Trucks broadcast their locations to fans on Twitter, and there are websites and apps to help you find your favorite truck or see who's currently in your area.

C8 ✉ 61 Columbus Avenue/62nd Street ☎ 212/977-7700 🕐 Daily lunch and dinner 🚇 A, B, C, D 1 59th Street–Columbus Circle

## SCHILLERS $–$$

schillersny.com

The man who brought France to Manhattan (Balthazar, Pastis) veers toward the Mitteleuropa deli here.
G18 ✉ 131 Rivington Street/Norfolk Street ☎ 212/260-4555 🕐 Daily breakfast/brunch, lunch, dinner 🚇 F 2nd Avenue

## SERENDIPITY 3 $

serendipity3.com

This toy box cum candy store makes the original and best "Frozen Hot Chocolate," as well as burgers, soups and grills.
F9 ✉ 225 E 60th Street/2nd Avenue ☎ 212/838-3531 🕐 Daily lunch and dinner 🚇 4, 5, 6 59th Street

## THE SPOTTED PIG $$

thespottedpig.com

You may have to wait for a table (you can't reserve) at this Michelin-starred, Anglo-style gastro pub. Order the *gnudi*, a ricotta-spinach gnocchi that chef April Bloomfield has made her own.
D16 ✉ 314 W 11th Street/Greenwich Avenue ☎ 212/620-0393 🕐 Daily lunch and dinner, Sat–Sun also brunch 🚇 1 Christopher Street

## SSÄM BAR $$

ssambar.momofuku.com

This Korean eatery is part of chef David Chang's Momofuku empire. The daily menu could offer anything from mason jars of kimchi to pork chops in Asian fish sauce.
F16 ✉ 207 Second Avenue/13th Street ☎ 212/254-3500 🕐 Daily lunch, dinner 🚇 L 3rd Avenue

### BAGEL PEOPLE

If NYC has a signature food, it might be the bagel. One top choice is Absolute Bagels (B2 ✉ 2788 Broadway/108th Street ☎ 212/932-2052), which serves classic flavors like sesame, pumpernickel, and poppy. To go truly old-school, visit Kossar's Bialys (G18 ✉ 367 Grand Street/Essex Street ☎ 212/473-4810), the only kosher purveyor of these oniony bagel-like breads still operating on the Lower East Side.

## UNCLE NICK'S $$

unclenicksgreekrestaurant.com

A fun atmosphere and hearty cooking are hallmarks at this friendly West Side Greek restaurant. The seafood is straight off the dock.
B10 ✉ 747 9th Avenue/50th Street ☎ 212/245-7992 🕐 Daily lunch and dinner 🚇 C, E 50th Street

## VEGETARIAN DIM SUM $

vegetariandimsum.com

Short on atmosphere but long on taste, this all-veggie dim sum parlor serves up creative fare at rock-bottom prices. On a cold day, try the excellent soups.
F20 ✉ 24 Pell Street/Doyers Street ☎ 212/577-7176 🕐 Daily lunch and dinner 🚇 N, R, Q, 6, J, Z Canal Street

## VESELKA $

veselka.com

Dine here at any time of day or night on Ukrainian and Polish soul food. The menu ranges from handmade *pierogi* (dumplings) to goulash and *blintzes*.
F16 ✉ 144 2nd Avenue/E 9th Street ☎ 212/228-9682 🕐 Daily 24 hours 🚇 6 Astor Place; F 2nd Avenue; R 8th Street

EAT

**149**

# Sleep

**With options ranging from the luxurious to simple budget hotels, New York has accommodations to suit everyone. In this section establishments are listed alphabetically.**

| | |
|---|---|
| Introduction | **152** |
| Directory | **153** |
| Sleeping A–Z | **153** |

SLEEP

# Introduction

There are plenty of hotel rooms but it is hard to find a comfortable room under $150. If money is no object, reserve a room at the Four Seasons.

### On a Budget

The fact of the matter is that lodging in New York on a budget can be tough and even budget chains can be pricey. Note that while outer-borough or airport hotels may be tempting, they can put you far away from sights and attractions. Many good hotels offer discounts: Monitor booking websites assiduously or consider a hotel alternative (▷ panel, below).

### Luxury Living

You'll find first-class luxury hotels throughout the city, although many are in Midtown. Nearly every hotel room comes with air-conditioning, private bathroom, coffeemaker, cable TV, telephone and hair dryer as standard, but top-class hotel rooms also boast luxe fabrics and linens, high-tech electronics and high staff-to-guest ratios.

### Prices

Today there is no such thing as a standard rack rate. Prices change with customer demand, so call the hotel and ask about the best available rate and special discounts. Alternatively, go online to discount services hotels.com, quikbook.com or hoteldiscounts.com. Note that taxes will be added to your bill, plus a daily occupancy fee.

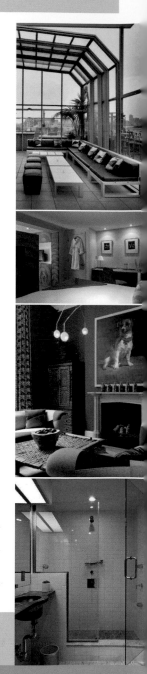

### HOME AWAY FROM HOME

One way to stretch your travel budget is to consider a home stay or apartment swap. HomeExchange.com (for a fee) will help you swap homes with New Yorkers. VRBO.com is another reputable source for short-term apartment rentals.

*From top: The Plunge Bar and Lounge at Hotel Gansevoort; guest room in the Shoreham; Crosby Street Hotel; clean lines at the Shoreham*

SLEEP

# Directory

## Lower Manhattan

**Budget**
Cosmopolitan
**Mid-Range**
Off Soho Suites
**Luxury**
Crosby Street Hotel
Ritz-Carlton Battery Park

## Downtown and Chelsea

**Budget**
Carlton Arms
Hotel 17
**Mid-Range**
Maritime Hotel
Washington Square
**Luxury**
Hotel Gansevoort
Inn at Irving Place

## Midtown

**Budget**
Ameritania Hotel
Hotel Wolcott

**Mid-Range**
70 Park Avenue
Algonquin Hotel
Casablanca
The Hudson
Jolly Madison Hotel
Library Hotel
Millennium Broadway
The Time
**Luxury**
Four Seasons
Mandarin Oriental
The Plaza
St. Regis
The Shoreham

## Upper West Side

**Budget**
Hotel Belleclaire
**Mid-Range**
Excelsior
Hotel Beacon

# Sleeping A–Z

| PRICES |
| --- |
| Prices are approximate and based on a double room for one night. |

| | |
| --- | --- |
| $$$ | over $400 |
| $$ | $201–$400 |
| $ | $100–$200 |

### 70 PARK AVENUE $$
70parkave.com
The first foray into New York by boutique hotel pioneers Kimpton, this 205-room Murray Hill place has a quietly contemporary decor, luxurious extras such as touch-screen room service, a pillow menu, good sound systems and a special yoga channel on the huge flatscreen TV.

E12   70 Park Avenue/38th Street
212/973-2400   Silverleaf Tavern
4, 5, 6, 7, S Grand Central–42nd Street

### ALGONQUIN HOTEL $$
algonquinhotel.com
The Algonquin is forever associated with the only group of literary wits to be named after a piece of furniture: The Algonquin Round Table. The bon viveurs achieved almost as much at the bar here as they did in the the pages of the embryonic *New Yorker*, with Robert Benchley, Dorothy Parker

and Alexander Woolcott well ensconced. The Rose Room still contains the very table they sat at.
➕ D11 ✉ 59 W 44th Street ☎ 212/840-6800 🚇 B, D, F, M 42nd Street–Bryant Park, 7 5th Avenue

## AMERITANIA HOTEL $

ameritaniahotelnewyork.com
If you want to be in the heart of the theater district then the Ameritania provides mid-class accommodation with the added benefit of spacious common areas and lounge bar.
➕ C10 ✉ 230 W 54th Street/Broadway ☎ 407/740-6442 🚇 N, Q, R 57th Street–7th Avenue

## CARLTON ARMS $

carltonarms.com
Decorated with crazy murals in the lobby and some rooms, this is one of New York's wackiest hotels. Amenities are minimal but there is a communal atmosphere that makes travelers feel at home. As it says on the business card, "this ain't no Holiday Inn." The 54 comfortable rooms offer good value.
➕ F14 ✉ 160 E 25th Street/Lexington–3rd avenues ☎ 212/679-0680 🚇 6 23rd Street

## CASABLANCA $$

casablancahotel.com
Moroccan prints and tiles make this small boutique hotel an oasis of color and style. Rooms range from cozy classics to premium kings and mini-suites, all with luxurious bath amenities and complimentary WiFi. Deluxe continental breakfast and passes to New York Sports Club are included.
➕ D11 ✉ 147 W 43rd Street/7th Avenue ☎ 212/869-1212 🚇 N, Q, R, S, 1, 2, 3, 7, 9 Times Square–42nd Street

## COSMOPOLITAN $

cosmohotel.com
No frills in any sense of the word exist at this 150-room, seven-story block in Tribeca. But, if you reckon the real estate rule applies to hotels, you'll love it—the location, location, location is prime. The clean, fully functional rooms vary a good deal in size, so if the hotel isn't full and you're not happy with

*The bar in Crosby Street Hotel, a fashionable choice in SoHo*

*The Ty Warner Penthouse in the Four Seasons*

the room you are shown, ask to
see another one.

🔲 E20 ✉ 95 W Broadway/Chambers
Street ☎ 212/566-1900 🚇 A, C Chambers
Street

### CROSBY STREET HOTEL $$$

crosbystreethotel.com

This new kid on the block is from
über-cool hoteliers Firmdale. In the
heart of vibrant SoHo, the 86
rooms and suites over 11 floors
have full-length warehouse-style
windows. The interior design by Kit
Kemp is fresh and contemporary,
and the hotel has a gym, cinema
and a sculpture garden, as well as
a selection of one- and two-bed-
room suites.

🔲 E18 ✉ 79 Crosby Street, between
Prince and Spring streets ☎ 212/226-6400
🚇 4, 6 Spring Street–Lafayette Street

### EXCELSIOR $$

excelsiorhotelny.com

The location is quite fabulous—
steps from Central Park and the
American Museum of Natural
History, with the subway practically
underfoot. The building is grand,
too, heavy on the wood paneling,
faux-oils and gilt frames. Rooms,
though not beautiful in generic
brocades and stripes, are fine;
even some standard rooms over-
look the park.

🔲 C6 ✉ 45 W 81st Street/Columbus
☎ 212/362-9200 🚇 B, C 81st Street–
Museum of Natural History

### FOUR SEASONS $$$

fourseasons.com/newyork

The grandiose I.M. Pei building
makes a big first impression—all
towering lobbies, marble and mezzanine lounges. The rooms don't
disappoint. In beiges and creams,
they're big, with tons of closets,
tubs that fill in no time and, in
some, great views. Many consider
this Manhattan's top hotel.

🔲 E9 ✉ 57 E 57th Street, Park–Madison
avenues ☎ 212/758-5700 🍴 The Garden,
L'Atelier de Joël Robuchon 🚇 N, R 5th
Avenue

### HOTEL 17 $

hotel17ny.com

The kitschy decor almost seems
deliberate—its stripey wallpaper,
floral bedspread, nylon carpet look
seems to hit a chord with rock 'n'
roll types and models. That could
also be on account of its brownstone Gramercy Park location and
low rates, of course. It offers
shared or private baths.

🔲 F15 ✉ 225 E 17th Street/2nd–3rd avenues ☎ 212/475-2845 🚇 L 3rd Avenue

### HOTEL BEACON $$

beaconhotel.com

In the middle of Broadway, on the
Upper West Side, the Beacon feels
more like an apartment building
than a hotel. Some of the 200-
plus rooms here have kitchenettes.

🔲 B7 ✉ 2130 Broadway/75th Street
☎ 212/787-1100 🚇 1, 2, 3 72nd Street

**SLEEP**

---

**B&BS**

Those who'd like to experience the city more like a local may opt to stay in a B&B, of
which there are plenty in all five boroughs. Often located in historic brownstones in
charming neighborhoods, many offer great prices. (Be aware, however, that some B&Bs
don't actually include the second B, breakfast.) Visit bedandbreakfast.com/new-york-city-
new-york.html for listings.

*Rooftop pool at Hotel Gansevoort*

### HOTEL BELLECLAIRE $

hotelbelleclaire.com

Mark Twain lived here, as did Maxim Gorky. Now the early-20th-century building offers 230 clean, minimal guest rooms, with pine furniture and pale apricot-color walls, though only the rooms with shared bathrooms are budget.

➕ B6 ✉ 250 W 77th Street/Broadway ☎ 212/362-7700 🚇 1 79th Street

### HOTEL GANSEVOORT $$$

hotelgansevoort.com

Fashion-obsessed young creatives consider this illuminated glass tower style-central. The stark guest rooms are furnished in stone and sand colors and equipped with lots of high-tech gadgets. Facilities include a rooftop pool, a spa, the

Provocateur Nightclub, and the Plunge restaurant and bar.

➕ C16 ✉ 18 9th Avenue/13th Street ☎ 212/206-6700 🚇 A, C, E 14th Street; L 8th Avenue

### HOTEL WOLCOTT $

wolcott.com

Within walking distance of Macy's and the Empire State Building, this hotel is great value for money. It has comfortable rooms with private bath and even offers free morning coffee and muffins.

➕ D13 ✉ 4 W 31st Street, between 5th Avenue and Broadway ☎ 212/268-2900 🚇 B, D, F, M, N, Q, R 34th Street–Herald Square

### THE HUDSON $$

hudsonhotel.com

All subdued lighting and minimalist chic, the Hudson is a short hop from Central Park and a subway stop with good connections. It comes alive at night with a popular bar and there is a basement gym. Request a room (tiny, even by NY standards) overlooking the atrium, as these tend to be quieter.

➕ B9 ✉ 356 W 58th Street/Columbus Avenue ☎ 212/554-6000 🚇 1, A, C, B, D 59th Street–Columbus Circle

### INN AT IRVING PLACE $$$

innatirving.com

With just 12 guest rooms and junior suites, this discreet hotel (there's no name outside) is set in

---

## LOCATION, LOCATION, LOCATION

Thinking about how you plan to spend your time in New York can help you find the best neighborhood in which to stay. Seeing theater every night? A hotel within walking distance of Times Square will be a real plus. Love people watching? The Upper West Side is great for strolling and hotels are within easy reach of Central Park. Shopping? Check out a Lower Manhattan hotel near SoHo's many stores.

two 1830s town houses near Gramercy Park, with elegant decor, period furniture, open fireplaces and a romantic atmosphere.
✛ E15  ✉ 56 Irving Place/17th Street
☎ 212/533-4600  🚇 4, 5, 6, L, N, Q, R 14th Street–Union Square

### JOLLY MADISON HOTEL $$

jollymadison.com
This is a very charming Italian-run boutique hotel located on Madison Avenue. It has warmth, elegance and style, but what sets it apart is a blend of 1920s American architecture and modern facilities coupled with extremely comfortable and spacious rooms.
✛ E12  ✉ 22 E 38th Street/Madison
☎ 212/802-0600  🚇 B, D, F, M 42nd Street–Bryant Square

### LIBRARY HOTEL $$

libraryhotel.com
Each of the 10 floors of the hotel is dedicated to one of the 10 subject categories from the Dewey Decimal System and each room has a collection of art and books related to a subcategory.

The interior is modern and minimalist.
✛ E11  ✉ 299 Madison Avenue/41st Street
☎ 212/983-4500  🚇 S, 4, 5, 6, 7 Grand Central–42nd Street

### MANDARIN ORIENTAL $$$

mandarinoriental.com/newyork
The best of the 248 rooms and suites have lovely panoramic views across Central Park or over the Hudson.
✛ C9  ✉ 80 Columbus Circle/60th Street
☎ 212/805-8800  🍴 Asiate  🚇 A, C, B, D, 1 59th Street–Columbus Circle

### MARITIME HOTEL $$

themaritimehotel.com
Super-hip trendsters will love this quirky 120-room place in the thick of the Meatpacking District. Porthole windows facing the Hudson and navy-blue soft furnishings add to the ship-like feel of the small rooms. It also has a fitness center, a happening bar scene and an Asian-fusion restaurant.
✛ C15  ✉ 363 W 16th Street/9th Avenue
☎ 212/242-4300  🍴 Tao Downtown
🚇 A, C, E 14th Street

**SLEEP**

View over the Hudson and Central Park from The Mandarin Oriental

### MILLENNIUM BROADWAY $$

millenniumhotels.com

The Millennium is a good choice for theater-lovers as it's walking distance from 40 Broadway shows and several off-Broadway theaters, as well as Times Square. The high-ceilinged lobby leads to a 52-story building, with 750 guest rooms, and suites that have floor-to-ceiling windows for great views.

🚹 D11 ✉ 145 W 44th Street/Broadway ☎ 212/768-4400 🚇 1, 2, 3, 7, N, Q, R, S Times Square–42nd Street

### OFF SOHO SUITES $$

offsoho.com

Since opening twenty years ago, this hotel's very off-SoHo location (on the Lower East Side bordering Nolita) has become all the rage. The suites are mini-studio apartments with no decorative advantages whatsoever but with full kitchens, private phones and satellite TV. The Economy suites share a kitchen and bathroom.

🚹 F18 ✉ 11 Rivington Street/Bowery ☎ 212/979-9815 🚇 F 2nd Avenue; J, Z Bowery

### THE PLAZA $$$

plazany.com

With 180 guest rooms and 102 luxury suites, overlooking either Fifth Avenue or Central Park, the Plaza is one of the most expensive hotels in the city. An array of Eloise-themed options are available for fans of Kay Thompson's diminutive heroine.

🚹 D9 ✉ 5th Avenue at Central Park South ☎ 212/759-3000 🚇 N, Q, R 5th Avenue–59th Street

### RITZ-CARLTON BATTERY PARK $$$

ritzcarlton.com

This glass-sided tower has one thing no other hotel has: views of New York Harbor. Decor is pale and contemporary, and the service and facilities are exemplary.

🚹 D23 ✉ 2 West Street/Battery Place ☎ 212/344-0800 🚇 1 South Ferry

### ST. REGIS $$$

stregisnewyork.com

Offering Louis XV style in the middle of Midtown, this hotel has 229 extremely plush rooms and

*The St. Regis, a luxurious option in Midtown*

suites and gives discreet service, with a butler available 24 hours.
➕ E9–E10 ✉ 2 E 55th Street/5th Avenue ☎ 212/753-4500 🚇 E, M 5th Avenue–53rd Street

### THE SHOREHAM $$$

shorehamhotel.com

The sleek Shoreham Hotel, behind the Museum of Modern Art, has 177 small but nice rooms and suites, with suede walls, diffused lighting and soft white comforters on the beds. The choice rooms are at the back of the hotel. Extras such as Aveda products, free round-the-clock coffee and a hotel-curated art gallery, plus high-end technology in the better rooms add good value.
➕ D10 ✉ 33 W 55th Street/5th–6th avenues ☎ 855/212-6773 🚇 B, Q 57th Street

### THE TIME $$

thetimeny.com

Just off Times Square, the 164 rooms and 28 suites sport bold, primary colors. Choose a red, yellow or blue room and you'll find that color not only covering the bed and selected wall parts but also appearing in candy and scent form. A Bose radio and Molton Brown toiletries add value but can't make the small rooms grow any larger, though you can spread out a bit in the small gym and rather swank lounge and restaurant.

➕ C11 ✉ 224 W 49th Street/between Broadway and 8th Avenue ☎ 212/246-5252 🚇 N, Q, R, S, 1, 2, 3, 7 Times Square–42nd Street

### WASHINGTON SQUARE $$

washingtonsquarehotel.com

The only hotel in the heart of Greenwich Village has long been a favorite of musicians, writers and artists. The smart, comfortable rooms have retro furniture, while the beautiful lobby has a bright 1930s Parisian air and friendly staff. Extras include complimentary breakfast, WiFi and gym; and there are two bars and the North Square restaurant (▷ 147).
➕ E16 ✉ 103 Waverley Place/MacDougal Street ☎ 212/777-9515 🍽 North Square restaurant 🚇 A, C, E, B, D, F, M 4th Street–Washington Square

*The Shoreham's bar*

**SLEEP**

# Need to Know

**This section takes you through all the practical aspects of your trip to make it run more smoothly and to give you confidence before you go and while you are there.**

Planning Ahead                162
Getting There                 164
Getting Around                166
Essential Facts               168
Books and Films               171

# Planning Ahead

## WHEN TO GO

Fall is generally thought the best time to visit New York. In August many New Yorkers are driven out of town by the searing heat. However, during this time lines are shorter, restaurant reservations easier and outdoor festivals at their peak. The city has occasional blizzards in winter, but these rarely cause disruption.

### TIME

New York is on Eastern Standard Time, three hours ahead of Los Angeles and five hours behind the UK.

### TEMPERATURE

| JAN | FEB | MAR | APR | MAY | JUN | JUL | AUG | SEP | OCT | NOV | DEC |
|-----|-----|-----|-----|-----|-----|-----|-----|-----|-----|-----|-----|
| 39°F | 41°F | 46°F | 61°F | 70°F | 81°F | 84°F | 82°F | 77°F | 66°F | 54°F | 39°F |
| 4°C | 5°C | 8°C | 16°C | 21°C | 27°C | 29°C | 28°C | 25°C | 19°C | 12°C | 4°C |

**Spring** (March to May) is unpredictable—even in April snow showers can alternate with shirtsleeves weather—but the worst of winter is over by mid-March.

**Summer** (June to August) can be extremely hot and humid, especially July and August, when the heat can make sightseeing exhausting.

**Fall** (September to November) sees warm temperatures persisting into October.

**Winter** (December to February) can be severe, with heavy snow, biting winds and subfreezing temperatures.

### WHAT'S ON

**January/February** *Chinese New Year* (Chinatown).
**February** *Westminster Kennel Club Dog Show* (☎ 212/213-3165).
**March 17** *St. Patrick's Day Parade* (5th Avenue, 44th–86th streets).
**March/April** *Easter Parade* (5th Avenue, 44th–57th streets).
**April–October** *Baseball season.*
**May** *9th Avenue International Food Festival* (9th Avenue, 37th–57th streets ☎ 212/581-7217).
**June** *Metropolitan Opera park concerts* (☎ 212/362-6000). *Lesbian and Gay Pride*

*Parade* (52nd Street and 5th Avenue to Christopher and Greenwich streets).
**June–September** *Shakespeare in the Park* (Delacorte Theater ☎ 212/539-8750). *NY Philharmonic park concerts.*
**July 4** *Independence Day.*
**July–August** *Harlem Week* (☎ 212/862-8477). *Lincoln Center Out-of-Doors Festival* (☎ 212/875-5000).
**August–September** *US Open Tennis Championships* (☎ 718/760-6200).
**September** *Feast of San Gennaro* (Little Italy).

**September–October** *New York Film Festival* (Lincoln Center ☎ 212/875-5601).
**October** *Columbus Day Parade* (5th Avenue, 44th–79th streets).
**November** *NYC Marathon* (Staten Island to Central Park, nycmarathon.org). *Macy's Thanksgiving Day Parade* (✉ Central Park West, 77th Street ☎ 212/494-4495).
**December** *Tree Lighting Ceremony* (✉ Rockefeller Center ☎ 212/332-6868). *New Year's Eve celebrations* (✉ Times Square).

## NEW YORK ONLINE

### nycgo.com
The official tourism website, linked to the NYC Information Center in Midtown, includes a calendar of events, accommodations information, news updates and lots more. The helpful trip-planning section includes themed itineraries.

### broadway.org
The Broadway League's official site, with up-to-date information on shows, theaters and the theater district in several languages.

### newyorkcityanswers.com
Want to know what books to read before you get to the city? Which are the best tours? Tips and tricks from native New Yorkers? This aptly named site tells all.

### nyc.gov
As the official homepage of the City of New York, the site offers links to the Office of the Mayor as well as information about community services, legal policies, city agencies, news and weather and visitor information.

### nyc-arts.org
With a comprehensive calendar ranging for lectures about architecture to whether the circus is in town, NYC-ARTS lives up to its catchphrase as "the complete guide."

### nymag.com
One of the most comprehensive websites covering what's on in the city, including good restaurant reviews.

### nytimes.com
Here you'll get an inside look at New York from one of the world's most respected newspapers. The site has links to sections covering everything from world affairs to sports.

### timessquare.com
All about Times Square and the area around, Broadway and its theaters in particular, with booking information.

## TRAVEL SITES

**fodors.com**
A complete travel-planning site. You can research prices and weather, book air tickets, cars and rooms, pose questions to fellow travelers and find links to other sites.

**iloveny.com**
Official NY State site. Information about touring the city and beyond.

**mta.info**
The Metropolitan Transportation Authority updates you on service changes and disruptions, and answers questions about buses and the subway.

## INTERNET ACCESS

WiFi is becoming more ubiquitous in New York all the time (in parks, cafés, libraries and most hotels), but it's still remarkable how many places aren't equipped—or charge a fee. Check nycgo.com/articles/wifi-in-nyc for up-to-date information. The MTA is bringing WiFi to many subway stations; look for the logo as you enter the station. The subways themselves aren't equipped...at least not yet.

# Getting There

## ARRIVING BY LAND

● Greyhound buses from across the US and Canada and commuter buses from New Jersey arrive at the Port Authority Terminal (✉ 625 8th Avenue ☎ 212/564-8484, greyhound.com).

● Commuter trains use Grand Central Terminal (✉ E 42nd Street/Park Avenue ☎ 212/532-4900).

● Long-distance trains arrive at Pennsylvania Station (✉ 31st Street/ 8th Avenue).

## CUSTOMS

● Non-US citizens may import duty-free: 1 liter of alcohol (this is the total allowance for wine and/or spirits), 200 cigarettes or 50 cigars and $100 of gifts. (No one under 21 can import alcohol.)

● Among restricted items for import are meat, fruit, plants, seeds and certain prescription medicines without a prescription or written statement from your doctor.

## SECURITY

● Always allow plenty of time for clearing security when arriving in or departing from the US.

## AIRPORTS

New York has three airports—John F. Kennedy (JFK) (✉ Queens, 15 miles/24km east of Manhattan ☎ 718/244-4444), Newark (✉ New Jersey, 16 miles/25km west ☎ 973/961-6000) and LaGuardia (✉ Queens, 8 miles/13km east ☎ 718/533-3400). Most international flights arrive at JFK. For details, visit panynj.gov.

**LaGuardia Airport**
8 miles (13km) to city center. Bus/minibus 40–45 minutes, $14

**Manhattan**

24km (15 miles)
16km (10 miles)
8km (5 miles)

**Newark Liberty International Airport**
16 miles (25km) to city center. Bus/minibus 40 minutes, $21

**J.F.K. International Airport**
15 miles (24km) to city center. Bus/minibus 1 hour, $16

### ENTRY REQUIREMENTS

Visitors to New York from outside the US must have a full passport valid for the length of their stay and a return ticket. Under the Visa Waiver Program (VWP), visitors from most European countries, Australia, New Zealand, Japan and others do not need a visa to enter the US for stays of up to 90 days. For a full, current list of these countries check the US State Department website travel.state.gov, under "US Visas."

All VWP visitors must have machine-readable passports, and all passports issued or renewed after October 26, 2006 must be e-passports containing additional biometric information. Children and infants must each have their own passport; they cannot be included on a parent's passport.

All visitors are required to obtain an electronic authorization to travel at least 72 hours prior to departure. Registration must be done under the Electronic System for Travel Authorization (ESTA™), part of the US Department of Homeland Security. (Visitors who possess a current, valid visa do not need to fill out the ESTA™ application.) Visitors who do not obtain ESTA™ clearance at least

72 hours in advance can be denied boarding or entry to the US. For more information and to fill out the application (in several languages), go to the ESTA™ website: esta.cdp.dhs.gov/esta. Further information is available on: cbp.gov/travel/international-visitors/esta.

There is a $14 fee payable for the ESTA™ authorization for all visitors in the VWP (▷ panel, right). Payment must be made by credit or debit card when filling out the application online. The authorization is valid for two years from the date of arrival in the US.

### FROM JFK
The journey to Manhattan takes around an hour. NYC Airporter express bus (tel 718/ 777-5111) runs every 20–30 minutes, 5am–11.30pm ($16). The SuperShuttle (▷ panel, right) runs to Manhattan 24 hours a day ($20). To reserve a place, use the courtesy telephone next to the Ground Transportation Desk. Taxis cost $52 plus tolls and tip; use the official taxi stand. The AirTrain to Jamaica (E, J, Z subway and Long Island Railroad) or Howard Beach (A subway) costs $5 and takes 12 minutes, plus 35–75 minutes to Midtown. It runs every 5–10 minutes, 24 hours a day.

### FROM NEWARK
It takes approximately 40 to 60 minutes to Manhattan. AirTrain (tel 888/397-4636) goes direct from all terminals 24 hours a day to Newark airport station, from which NJ Transit operates to Penn Station in Manhattan. SuperShuttle (▷ panel, right) runs a minibus to Midtown 24 hours a day ($21). A taxi costs $50–$80, plus tolls and a $15 surcharge from Manhattan.

### FROM LAGUARDIA
The journey from LaGuardia Airport to Manhattan takes between 40 and 60 minutes. SuperShuttle (▷ panel, right) runs a shared minibus 24 hours (cost $18). Services to Manhattan are also provided by NYC Airporter (cost $14; ▷ above). Taxis cost $25–$37 to Manhattan, plus tolls and tip.

### SUPERSHUTTLE
The SuperShuttle is a shared van service that offers efficient and inexpensive door-to-door service from New York's major airports to hotels, businesses and private residences throughout the city. You may have a slightly longer journey time if your stop is at the end of the driver's route, but the set fare can be less than half the cost of a taxi. It is not essential to book in advance; you can simply turn up at the Ground Transportation Desk and wait for the next available shuttle. However, booking in advance online saves time at the airport. You can also book by phone, and ask about any special promotional discounts that may apply:
☎ 1-800 258-3826, supershuttle.com.

# Getting Around

## LOST PROPERTY

● You are unlikely to recover items, but try the following (or call 311, city helpline):

**Subway and bus**
☎ 212/712-4500
**Taxi**
☎ 311
**JFK**
☎ 718/244-4225
**LaGuardia**
☎ 718/662-5043
**Newark**
☎ 907/787-0667
Report a loss quickly if claiming on your insurance.

## SUBWAY TIPS

● If your Metrocard doesn't work, don't go to a different turnstile or you'll lose a fare. As the display says, you should "swipe again."
● Check the circular signs on the outside of the cars to make sure you're boarding the correct train. Often two lines share a platform.
● Look at the boards above your head to check whether you're on the up- or down-town side and/or on the local or express track.

## TAXIS

**NYC–Licenced Taxis**
nyc.gov/taxi
**Carmel Car and Limousine**
☎ 212/666-6666
**Dial 7 Car and Limousine**
☎ 212/777-7777

## BUSES

● Bus stops are near corners, marked by a sign and a yellow painted curb. Any ride costs the same as the subway–use a Metrocard or correct change ($2.75; $3 single ride; coins only).
● Bus maps are available from token booth clerks in subway stations.
● Buses are safe and clean but can be very slow during rush hour. The fastest are Select Buses. For these limited-stop buses, swipe your Metrocard at the fare kiosk before boarding.
● If you pay by Metrocard you may transfer free from bus to subway or bus to bus within two hours of the time you paid the fare.

## SUBWAY

● New York subway lines often close or are diverted for maintenance on weekends, especially in Lower Manhattan and Brooklyn. Check the latest information (24 hours) before you travel (tel 511 or 718/330-1234, mta. info). New York's subway has 24 routes and 468 stations, many open 24 hours (those with a green globe outside are always staffed).
● Visit tripplanner.mta.info for accurate point-to-point subway directions.
● To ride the subway you need a Metrocard, which you can refill. Swipe the card to enter the turnstile. Refillable Metrocards are more economical than buying single-ride tickets, and you can share the card with a companion. You can top up the card at ticket machines inside the stations for any amount. The best deal are weekly or monthly unlimited ride Metrocards, but these cannot be shared.
● Many stations have separate entrances for up- and downtown services, often on opposite corners of the street. Check the subway map and listen to the platform announcements to determine if a train is local or express and will stop at your station.
● Children under 44in (113cm) tall ride free.
● Subways run all night, with many lines (such as the 1, 2, 3, 4, 5, 6) still crowded until well after midnight. Late-night riders should avoid less popular routes and always stay in the "off hour waiting area" until the train arrives.

## TAXIS

● The ubiquitous yellow cab is a New York trademark and, except possibly on very wet or busy evenings, very easy to hail. Hotel concierges can arrange and most bars, restaurants and nightspots will be able to assist. If you want to book something in advance try one of the companies in the Taxis panel (left).

● Cab drivers are notorious for (a) knowing nothing about New York geography, (b) not speaking English, and (c) having an improvisational driving style.

● Tip at least 15 percent. Bills larger than $10 are unpopular for short journeys.

## DRIVING

● Driving in New York is not to be recommended.

● The address of the nearest major car-rental outlet can be found by calling the following toll-free numbers:

Avis, tel 800/331-1212
Budget, tel 800/527-0700
Hertz, tel 800/654-3131
National, tel 877/222-9058.

● If driving in New York is unavoidable, make sure you understand the restrictions because penalties for infringements are stringent.

● In many streets parking alternates daily from one side to the other and it is illegal to park within 10ft (3m) either side of a fire hydrant. A car illegally parked will be towed away and the driver heavily fined. Parking is expensive.

● Within the city limits the speed limit is 25mph (40kph); right turns at a red light are prohibited.

● Passing a stopped school bus is illegal and stiff fines can be imposed.

## WALKING

New York is a great city for walking. If the weather is dry (if it isn't, umbrella vendors soon materialize), it's far nicer (and often faster) to hike a 10- or 20-block distance than to take the subway, or sit in a cab or bus stalled in traffic. To work it out, figure one minute per short block (north–south) and four per long block (east–west, on cross streets).

### OUTER BOROUGHS

Subway lines that appear to be identical in Manhattan often diverge in other boroughs, so make certain you know which line goes to your stop. Every major subway line goes through Manhattan except the G, which serves Queens and Brooklyn exclusively.

### VISITORS WITH DISABILITIES

City law requires that all facilities constructed after 1987 provide complete access to people with disabilities. Many owners of older buildings have willingly added disability-access features as well. Two important resources are the Mayor's Office for People with Disabilities (✉ 100 Gold Street, 2nd floor, 10038 ☎ 212/639-9675, nyc.gov/mopd) and Hospital Audiences' guide to New York's cultural insti-tutions, *Access for All* (☎ 212/575-7676, hainyc.org). This online guide describes the accessi-bility of each place, with information on hearing and visual aids, alternative entrances and the height of telephones and water fountains. HA also provides descriptions of theater performances for people with visual impairments.

# Essential Facts

## VISITOR INFORMATION

The city runs visitor information centers and kiosks around town. The most comprehensive is at Macy's ⊠ Herald Square ☎ 212/404-1222, nycgo. com ◷ Mon–Fri 9–7, Sat 10–7, Sun 11–7.
Touch screens allow visitors to research attractions and the center offers discount coupons, including to Macy's.

## EMERGENCY NUMBERS

● Police, Fire Department, Ambulance ☎ 911
● Crime Victims Hotline ☎ 212/577-7777
● Sex Crimes Report Line ☎ 212/267-7273

## ELECTRICITY
● The supply is 120 volts, 60 hz AC current.
● US appliances use flat two-prong plugs. European appliances require an adapter and a voltage transformer.

## ETIQUETTE
● Tipping: waitstaff get 15–20 percent (roughly double the 8.875 percent sales tax); so do cab drivers. Bartenders get about the same (though less than $1 is stingy). Bellhops ($1 per bag), room service waiters (10 percent) and hairdressers (15–20 percent) should also be tipped.
● There are stringent smoking laws in New York. Smoking is banned on public transportation, in cabs, in all places of work, including restaurants and bars, and, since 2011, in all city parks, on beaches and in Times Square.

## MAIL AND TELEPHONES
● The main post office (8th Avenue/33rd Street, tel 212/330-3296) is open daily. Visit usps.com to find neighborhood branches.
● Stamps are also available from hotel concierges, online at usps.com, at some delis and from vending machines in stores.
● All New York numbers require the area code (212, 718, 646, 347 or 917) when dialing. For long-distance calls, add 1 before the code.
● Hotels often levy surcharges for making calls.
● Foreign visitors: Watch out for mobile roaming charges that can result in a large bill on your return home; it's best to ask your mobile provider for information on data plans that can be used in the United States.
● To call the US from the UK, dial 001. To call the UK from the US, dial 011 44, then drop the first zero from the area code.

## MEDICAL TREATMENT
● It is essential to have adequate insurance.
● In the event of an emergency, the 911 operator will send an ambulance.
● Doctors on Call operate 24 hours (tel 212/737-1212).

• Near Midtown, 24-hour emergency rooms: Mt. Sinai Roosevelt Hospital, 10th Avenue and 59th Street, tel 212/523-4000.

• Dental Emergency Service, tel 646/837-7806. An operator will put you in touch with a dentist close to you open 24/7.

## MONEY MATTERS

• Credit cards are widely accepted. Visa, MasterCard, American Express, Diner's Card and Discover are the ones that are most commonly used.

• US dollar traveler's checks are hard to use outside hotels and currency exchange offices. It is difficult to exchange foreign currency traveler's checks, even at banks, and fees are high.

## NEWSPAPERS AND MAGAZINES

• The local papers are the *New York Times* (with a Sunday edition), the *Daily News* (also with Sunday supplements) and the *New York Post*. The free alternative paper the *Village Voice* includes extensive listings. The *Wall Street Journal*, once solely a financial daily, now covers the arts scene in New York on par with the *New York Times*.

• Pick up the *New Yorker* and *New York* magazine on newsstands; the glossier *In New York* and *Where* can be found in hotels and both showcase events.

• Monday to Friday, the free dailies *amNY* and *Metro New York* are handed out at virtually every Manhattan subway station, and have both news and event listings.

## OPENING HOURS

• Banks: Mon–Fri 9–3 or 3.30; some are open longer, and on Saturday.

• Stores: Mon–Sat 10–6; many are open far later, and on Sunday 12–6; those in the Village, Nolita and SoHo open and close later.

• Museums: hours vary, but Monday is the most common closing day.

• Post offices: Mon–Fri 8 or 9–6. Some open Sat 9–4.

• Opening times given are for general guidance only.

---

### MONEY

The unit of currency is the dollar (= 100 cents). Bills (notes) come in denominations of $1, $2, $5, $10, $20, $50 and $100; coins come in 25¢ (a quarter), 10¢ (a dime), 5¢ (a nickel) and 1¢ (a penny). Note: American coins are not marked with numerals (for example the 25 cent piece says "quarter dollar" only).

### TRAVEL INSURANCE

A minimum of $1 million medical cover is advised. Choose a policy that covers baggage and document loss, and cancellation.

### PUBLIC HOLIDAYS

• New Year's Day: January 1
• Martin Luther King, Jr. Day: third Monday of January
• Presidents' Day: third Monday of February
• Memorial Day: last Monday in May
• Independence Day: July 4
• Labor Day: first Monday in September
• Columbus Day: second Monday in October
• Veterans' Day: November 11
• Thanksgiving Day: fourth Thursday of November
• Christmas Day: December 25

## CONSULATES

**Australia**
✉ 150 E 42nd Street
☎ 212/351-6500
**Canada**
✉ 1251 6th Avenue
☎ 212/596-1759
**Denmark**
✉ 885 2nd Avenue,
18th Floor
☎ 212/223-4545
**France**
✉ 934 5th Avenue
☎ 212/606-3600
**Germany**
✉ 871 UN Plaza
☎ 212/610-9700
**Ireland**
✉ 345 Park Avenue
☎ 212/319-2555
**Italy**
✉ 690 Park Avenue
☎ 212/737-9100
**Norway**
✉ 825 3rd Avenue
☎ 646/430-7500
**Spain**
✉ 150 East 58th Street,
30th Floor
☎ 212/355/4080
**UK**
✉ 845 3rd Avenue
☎ 212/745-0200

## REST ROOMS

● Almost every department store has facilities, as do many smaller stores and key visitor attractions. Hotel lobbies, restaurants and bars offer rest rooms. Exercise caution when using facilities at public transportation hubs or in less salubrious neighborhoods.

## RADIO AND TELEVISION

● NY1 is the main cable channel serving the New York boroughs and will give you access to news, weather and travel as well as its own take on daily life in the Big Apple.
● WNYC (New York Public Radio) on 93.9 FM and 820 AM has news, culture and music items.
● Many TV shows are filmed in New York, from *Good Morning America* to the *The Daily Show*. Go to nycgo.com/tv-show-tapings for further details.

## SENSIBLE PRECAUTIONS

● Maintain awareness of your surroundings and of other people, and try to look as though you know your way around.
● Avoid the quieter subway lines at night and also certain areas of Brooklyn. Areas of Manhattan once considered unsafe (Alphabet City east of Avenue C, the far west of Midtown, north of about 110th Street and Central Park) are less edgy than they used to be. Still, keep your wits about you in deserted areas.
● Conceal your wallet; keep the fastener of your bag on the inside; and don't flash large amounts of cash or jewelry.

## STUDENTS

● An International Student Identity Card (ISIC) is good for reduced admission at many museums, theaters and other attractions.
● Carry the ISIC or some other photo ID card to prove you're a fulltime student or over 21.
● Under-25s will find it expensive to rent a car.

## VISITOR PASSES

Two visitor passes offer big savings if you're planning to take in multiple attractions:
● New York CityPass ($114 adults, $89 children, citypass.com) is valid for nine days and covers six top attractions, including the Statue of Liberty, Empire State Building and major museums.
● With the Explorer Pass (from $76 adults, $59 children, smartdestinations.com), you can choose 3, 5, 7, or 10 attractions from a list of 50 top sights and tours; valid for 30 days.

# Books and Movies

## BOOKS
### Non-fiction
- *The Historical Atlas of New York City* by Eric Homberger (1998), Henry Holt and Company.
- *Here is New York* by E.B. White (2000), Little Bookroom.
- *Inside the Apple: A Streetwise History of New York City* by Michelle and James Nevius (2009), Free Press.
- *The New York Nobody Knows: Walking 6,000 Miles in the City* (2013), Princeton University Press.
- *The New York Times' Book of New York* (2009), Black Dog & Leventhal Publishers.
- *Five Points* by Tyler Anbinder (2001), Free Press.

## MOVIES
*42nd Street* (1933), Lloyd Bacon
*King Kong* (1933), Merian C. Cooper
*Guys and Dolls* (1955), Joseph L. Mankiewicz
*An Affair to Remember* (1957), Leo McCarey
*Breakfast at Tiffany's* (1961), Blake Edwards
*West Side Story* (1961), Robert Wise
*The French Connection* (1971), William Friedkin
*Mean Streets* (1973), Martin Scorsese
*Taxi Driver* (1976), Martin Scorsese
*Saturday Night Fever* (1977), John Badham
*Manhattan* (1979), Woody Allen
*Broadway Danny Rose* (1984), Woody Allen
*The Cotton Club* (1984), Francis Ford Coppola
*Desperately Seeking Susan* (1985), Susan Seidelman
*Radio Days* (1987), Woody Allen
*Do the Right Thing* (1989), Spike Lee
*When Harry Met Sally* (1989), Rob Reiner
*A Bronx Tale* (1993), Robert De Niro
*Requiem for a Dream* (2000), Darren Aronofsky
*Gangs of New York* (2002), Martin Scorsese
*The Devil Wears Prada* (2006), David Franke
*Night at the Museum* (2006), Shawn Levy
*Julie and Julia* (2009), Nora Ephron
*The Adjustment Bureau* (2011) J.J. Abrams
*Bırdman: Or (The Unexpected Virtue of Ignorance)* (2014), Alejandro González Iñárritu
*The Intern* (2015), Nancy Meyers
*Brooklyn* (2015), John Crowley

### FICTION
F. Scott Fitzgerald's *The Beautiful and Damned* (1922), John Dos Passos's *Manhattan Transfer* (1925), J.D. Salinger's *The Catcher in the Rye* (1951) and Truman Capote's *Breakfast at Tiffany's* (1958) are all classic reads. Also recommended are Tom Wolfe's *Bonfire of the Vanities* (1987), *The New York Trilogy* (1988) by Paul Auster, and *New York: The Novel* (2010) by Edward Rutherfurd.

# Index

**A**

accommodations 150–159
airports 164–165
Alice Austen House 75
American Folk Art Museum 66
American Museum of Natural History 9, 14–15, 106
architecture 6–7

**B**

B&Bs 152, 155
banks 169
bars *see* entertainment
Battery Park 66
books and movies 171
Botanic Garden 17
Broadway 56–57, 129
Bronx Zoo 9, 74
Brooklyn 5, 11, 16–17, 108–109, 112, 167
Brooklyn Bridge 9, 66, 108
Brooklyn Bridge Park 17
Brooklyn Museum of Art 16–17
buses 164, 166

**C**

car rental 167
Castle Clinton National Monument 66
Central Park 9, 18–19, 96–97, 100, 102, 136
Chelsea Gallery District 66
Chinatown 20–21, 82
Chrysler Building 6, 9, 67
churches
  Grace Church 25, 68
  St. Patrick's Cathedral 71–72
  St. Patrick's Old Cathedral 72
  St. Paul's Chapel 72
  Trinity Church 59
City Hall 67
climate and seasons 162
The Cloisters 74
clubs 135
  *see also* entertainment
comedy clubs 128, 133, 134, 137
Coney Island 74–75
consulates 170
Cooper Hewitt Smithsonian Design Museum 22–23, 100
Cooper Union 23
credit cards 169
currency 169
customs regulations 164

**D**

David Geffen Hall 43, 133
dental services 169
disabilities, visitors with 167
Downtown and Chelsea 84–89
driving 167

**E**

East Village 24–25, 88
eating out 8, 138–149
Eldridge Street Synagogue 67
electricity 168
Electronic System for Travel Authorization (ESTA™) 164–165
Ellis Island 11, 26–27, 82
emergency telephone numbers 168
Empire State Building 6, 9, 28–29, 94
entertainment 9, 126–137
etiquette 168
events and festivals 162

**F**

Farther Afield 108–113
Federal Hall 59
Fifth Avenue 30–31, 94
Flatiron Building 6, 68
flea markets 117
Flushing Meadows-Corona Park 75
Frick Collection 32–33, 100

**G**

gardens and parks
  Battery Park 66
  Botanic Garden 17
  Brooklyn Bridge Park 17
  Central Park 18–19, 96–97, 100, 136
  High Line 40–41, 88
  Flushing Meadows-Corona Park 75
  Prospect Park 17
  Washington Square Park 37
GE Building 50, 51
Grace Church 25, 68
Grand Central Terminal 7, 34–35, 94, 145
greenmarket 125
Greenwich Village 36–37, 88
Guggenheim Museum 38–39, 100

**H**

harbor cruises 55, 129
Harlem 75
health 168

High Line 40–41, 88
Historic Richmond Town 75
history 10–11
hotels 150–159

**I**

insurance 168, 169
internet access 163
Italian American Museum 68

**J**

jazz 129, 132
Jewish Museum 68

**L**

Lincoln Center 42–43, 106
lost property 166
Lower East Side Tenement Museum 11, 68–69
Lower Manhattan 78–83

**M**

Mahayana Buddhist Temple 21
mail services 168
maps
  Downtown and Chelsea 86–87
  Farther Afield 110–111
  Lower Manhattan 80–81
  Midtown 92–93
  Upper East Side and Central Park 98–99
  Upper West Side 104–105
MCU Park 74
Meatpacking District 128
medical treatment 168–169
Merchant's House Museum 25
Met Breuer 69
Metropolitan Museum of Art 44–45, 100
Metropolitan Opera House 43, 135
Midtown 90–95
mobile phones 168
MoMA (Museum of Modern Art) 46–47, 94
money 169
Morgan Library and Museum 69
El Museo del Barrio 69
Museum of Arts and Design 70
Museum of Chinese in America 70
Museum of the City of New York 70
museums and galleries
  Alice Austen House 75

American Folk Art Museum 66
American Museum of Natural History 14–15, 106
Brooklyn Museum of Art 16–17
The Cloisters 74
Cooper Hewitt Smithsonian Design Museum 22–23, 100
Ellis Island 26–27
Frick Collection 32–33, 100
Guggenheim Museum 38–39, 100
Italian American Museum 68
Jewish Museum 68
Lower East Side Tenement Museum 11, 68–69
Merchant's House Museum 25
Met Breuer 69
Metropolitan Museum of Art 44–45, 100
Morgan Library and Museum 69
El Museo del Barrio 69
Museum of American Finance 59
Museum of Arts and Design 70
Museum of Chinese in America 70
Museum of Modern Art (MoMA) 46–47, 94
Museum of the City of New York 70
National Museum of the American Indian 73
National September 11 Memorial and Museum 62–63
Neue Galerie New York 70
New Museum of Contemporary Art 71
New-York Historical Society 71
New York Hall of Science 75
Queens Museum of Art 75
Rubin Museum of Art 71
Ukrainian Museum 25
Whitney Museum of American Art 60–61, 88

N
National Museum of the American Indian 73
National September 11 Memorial and Museum 62–63

NBC Studios 51
Neue Galerie New York 70
New Museum of Contemporary Art 8, 71
New York Aquarium 74
New York Hall of Science 75
New-York Historical Society 71
New York Public Library 7, 48–49, 94
New York Stock Exchange 58–59
newspapers and magazines 169
nightlife see entertainment
NoHo 24–25

O
One World Trade Center 5, 7, 63
opening hours 169

P
passports and visas 164
police 168
post offices 168, 169
Prospect Park 17
public holidays 169
public transportation 166–167

Q
Queens Museum of Art 75

R
radio and television 170
Radio City Music Hall 51, 136
restaurants 8, 141–149
rest rooms 170
Rockefeller Center 50–51, 94
Rubin Museum of Art 71

S
safety, personal 170
St. Patrick's Cathedral 71–72
St. Patrick's Old Cathedral 72
St. Paul's Chapel 7, 72
sales tax 140
sample sales 117, 123
shopping 8, 30–31, 114–125
   opening hours 169
skyscrapers 6–7
smoking 168
SoHo (South of Houston) 52–53, 82
SoHo Cast Iron Historic District 7, 52–53
South Street Seaport 7, 72
sports 9
Staten Island 75, 108
Statue of Liberty 11, 54–55, 82
Stonewall Inn 37
Strawberry Fields 19

students 170
subway 166

T
taxis 167
telephones 168
temperatures 162
theater tickets 56
time 162
Times Square 56–57, 94
tipping 140, 168
Top of the Rock 49
top tips 8–9
tours
   Downtown and Chelsea 84–89
   Farther Afield 108–113
   Lower Manhattan 78–83
   Midtown 90–95
   Upper East Side and Central Park 96–101
   Upper West Side 102–107
trains 164
Trinity Church 59
Trump Tower 73

U
Ukrainian Museum 25
Union Square 73
United Nations Headquarters 73
Upper East Side and Central Park 96–101
Upper West Side 102–107
U.S. Custom House 7, 73

V
views 8–9, 29, 51
visitor information 161–171
visitor passes 170

W
Wall Street 58–59, 82
Washington Memorial Arch 73
Washington Square 7, 73
Washington Square Park 37
websites 163
Whitney Museum of American Art 60–61, 88
World Trade Center 5, 11, 62–63, 82

Y
Yankee Stadium 75

Z
zoos 19, 74

The Automobile Association would like to thank the following photographers, companies and picture libraries for their assistance in the preparation of this book.

2(i-v) AA J Tims; 3(i-ii) AA/J Tims; 3(iii) Gansevoort Meatpacking NYC Gansevoort Meatpacking NYC; 3(iv) AA/J Tims; 4 AA/D Pollack; 5 AA/J Tims; 6t Nick Wood/Alamy; 6b, 6/7t, 6/7c AA/J Tims; 6/7b Photolibrary; 7t Photolibrary; 7tc AA/J Tims; 8t AA/C Sawyer; 8b Pablo Valentini/Alamy; 8/9t The Dinex Group Café Boulud NYC by B. Milne; 8/9b, 9t AA/J Tims; 9tc AA/J Tims; 9bc NYC images/Alamy; 9b AA/J Tims; 10l AA; 10r Mary Evans Picture Library/Classic Stock/H. Armstrong Roberts; 11l Mary Evans Picture Library; 11r Lower East Side Tenement Museum Courtesy the Lower East Side Tenement Museum, photography by Keiko Niwa; 12–14/5, 15, 16 AA/J Tims, 16/7t Michael Matthews /Alamy; 16–20 AA/J Tims; 21t AA/J Tims; 21bl AA/C Sawyer; 21br AA/J Tims; 22 Sandra Baker/Alamy; 23 AA/J Tims; 24 Tetra Images /Alamy; 24/5t AA/C Sawyer; 24/5b AA/ Simon McBride; 25t The Ukrainian Museum Courtesy of The Ukrainian Museum; 25b AA/C Sawyer; 26–29 AA/J Tims; 30b Patrick Batchelder/Alamy; 30t, 30/31, 31 AA/J Tims; 32/33 The Frick Collection, New York The Frick Collection, New York Photo: Michael Bodycomb 33 The Frick Collection, New York. The Frick Collection, New York Photo: Galen Lee. 34–37 AA/J Tims; 38/39 Christian Kober/Robert Harding; 39 AA/J Tims; 40 Douglas Lander /Alamy; 40/41 Chris A Selby/Alamy; 42/43 Lincoln Center Media Desk Photo Gallery. Photo credit: Mark Bussell Lincoln Center for the Performing Arts; 43t Lincoln Center Media Desk Photo Gallery. Photo credit: Stefan Cohen Lincoln Center for the Performing Arts; 43bl Lincoln Center Media Desk Photo Gallery. Photo credit: Stefan Cohen Lincoln Center for the Performing Arts; 43br Lincoln Center Media Desk Photo Gallery. Photo credit: Mark Bussell Lincoln Center for the Performing Arts; 44/45 AA/J Tims; 45tr AA/J Tims; 45br AA/J Tims; 46 AA/J Tims, Chagall®/© ADAGP, Paris and DACS, London 2011 AND © ADAGP, Paris and DACS, London 2011. 46/7 AA/J Tims; 48tl AA/J Tims; 46bl Michal Besser /Alamy; 48–55 AA/J Tims; 56t, b AA/J Tims; 56/7b PACIFIC PRESS/Alamy; 57tl, 57r AA/J Tims; 58–59 AA/J Tims; 60/61 The Bridgeman Art Library Dempsey and Firpo, Whitney Museum of American Art/Bridgeman; 61 Whitney Museum © Whitney Museum/Ed Lederman; 62l John Kellerman/Alamy; 62/63t Christopher Penler/Alamy; 62/63b David Cooper /Alamy; 63r Lenz/Alamy; 64 AA/J Tims; 66l American Folk Art Museum American Folk Art Museum; 66r AA/J Tims; 67 AA/J Tims; 68 Photolibrary; 69–71 AA/J Tims; 72 Getty Images Tetra Images/Getty Images; 73–74 AA/J Tims; 75 Photolibrary; 76 AA/J Tims; 78t AA/J Tims; 78b AA/J Tims; 79t AA/J Tims; 79b Spencer Grant /Alamy; 82(i-vi) AA/J Tims; 82(vii) John Kellerman /Alamy; 84t AA/J Tims; 84b AA/World Travel Library/Alamy; 85t AA/J Tims; 85b Aurora Photos /Alamy; 88(i, ii) AA/J Tims; 88(iii) Asia Photopress/Alamy; 88(iv) Robert Nickelsberg/Alamy; 90t AA/J Tims; 90b AA/Simon McBride; 91 AA/J Tims; 94 AA/J Tims; 96t AA/J Tims; 96b AA/J Tims; 97t AA/J Tims; 100(i) AA/J Tims; 100(ii) AA/C Sawyer; 100(iii) The Frick Collection, New York The Frick Collection, New York Photo: Michael Bodycomb; 100 AA/J Tims; 102t American Folk Art Museum American Folk Art Museum; 102b AA/J Tims; 103t Matthiola /Alamy; 103c AA/J Tims; 103b Lincoln Center Media Desk Photo Gallery. Photo credit: Mark Bussell Lincoln Center for the Performing Arts; 106 AA/J Tims; 107 AA/Simon McBride; 108t Prisma Bildagentur AG/Alamy; 108b AA/J Tims; 109t Alamy Richard Ellis/Alamy; 109b AA/J Tims; 112, 113, 114 AA/J Tims; 116/117t AA/J Tims; 116/117mt, mb AA/J Tims; 116/117b Richard Levine /Alamy; 117mt AA/J Tims; 117mb AA/C Sawyer; 119, 120, 123 AA/J Tims; 124 Yadid Levy/Alamy; 126 AA/J Tims; 128 Prisma Bildagentur AG/Alamy; 128/9t Jon Arnold Images Ltd /Alamy; 128/9tc AA/J Tims; 128/9bc Lincoln Center Media Desk Photo Gallery. Photo credit: Iwan BAA/n Lincoln Center for the Performing Arts; 128, 129, 131, 132 AA/J Tims; 136 AA/Paul Kenward; 138 AA/J Tims; 140t AA/J Tims; 140tc AA/C Sawyer; 140bc The Dinex Group Café Boulud NYC by B. Milne; 140b AA/J Tims; 143 AA/J Tims; 145 AA/Julian Love; 146 Kathy deWitt/Alamy; 150 Gansevoort Meatpacking NYC; 150 Gansevoort Meatpacking NYC; 152t Gansevoort Meatpacking NYC Gansevoort Meatpacking NYC 152tc Shoreham hotel; 152bc CROSBY STREET/ www.crosbystreethotel.com; 152b Shoreham hotel; 154l CROSBY STREET HOTEL/ www.crosbystreethotel.com; 154r Four Seasons Hotels and Resorts/Saylor, Durston Four Seasons Hotels and Resorts; 156 Gansevoort Meatpacking NYC Gansevoort Meatpacking NYC; 157 Mandarin Oriental, New York; 158 AA/C Sawyer; 159 Shoreham hotel; 160 AA/J Tims.

Every effort has been made to trace the copyright holders, and we apologise in advance for any unintentional omissions or errors. We would be pleased to apply any corrections in a following edition of this publication.

# New York City 25 Best

**WRITTEN BY** Kate Sekules
**ADDITIONAL WRITING BY** Donna Dailey
**UPDATED BY** James and Michelle Nevius
**SERIES EDITOR** Clare Ashton
**COVER DESIGN** Chie Ushio, Yuko Inagaki
**DESIGN WORK** Kat Mead
**IMAGE RETOUCHING AND REPRO** Ian Little

Published in the United Kingdom by AA Publishing

**ISBN 978-0-1475-4628-9**

**THIRTEENTH EDITION**

All details in this book are based on information supplied to us at press time. Always confirm information when it matters, especially if you're making a detour to visit a specific place. Fodor's expressly disclaims any liability, loss, or risk, personal or otherwise, that is incurred as a consequence of the use of any of the contents of this book.

**SPECIAL SALES**
This book is available for special discounts for bulk purchases for sales promotions or premiums. For more information, email specialmarkets@penguinrandomhouse.com.

Color separation by AA Digital Department
Printed and bound by Leo Paper Products, China

10 9 8 7 6 5 4 3 2 1

A05379
Maps in this title produced from mapping data supplied by Global Mapping, Brackley, UK © Global Mapping and data from openstreetmap.org
© OpenStreetMap contributors
Transport map © Communicarta Ltd, UK

# Titles in the Series

- Amsterdam
- Bangkok
- Barcelona
- Boston
- Brussels and Bruges
- Budapest
- Chicago
- Dubai
- Dublin
- Edinburgh
- Florence
- Hong Kong
- Istanbul
- Krakow
- Las Vegas
- Lisbon
- London
- Madrid
- Melbourne
- Milan
- Montréal
- Munich
- New York City
- Orlando
- Paris
- Rome
- San Francisco
- Seattle
- Shanghai
- Singapore
- Sydney
- Tokyo
- Toronto
- Venice
- Vienna
- Washington, D.C.